seebeyond

CLIFFORD GOLDSTEIN

See Beyond
Copyright © 2013 by Adventist Media Network.
See Beyond is part of the Beyond the Search® documentary project created by Adventist Media Network in Australia.

The author assumes full responsibility for the accuracy of all facts and quotations as cited in this book.

Bible quotations are taken from the Holy Bible, New King James Version.
Copyright © 1994, Thomas Nelson Publishers.

Proudly published and printed in Australia by

Warburton, Victoria

Edited by Nathan Brown and Talitha Simmons
Designed by Loopeck Lim and Kym Jackson
Cover photograph by urbancow/istockphoto.com
Cover design by Loopeck Lim
Typeset in in Univers 11/15
ISBN   978 1 921292 81 1 (print edition)
              978 1 921292 82 8 (ebook edition)

To order additional copies of this book or for more information, visit **www.beyond.info**

CONTENTS

Why 4

What's your story? 10
The great controversy 20
Another day in paradise 30
Truth happens 38
Where have all the heroes gone? 48
Rescue 58
Proof of guilt 68
Signs and laws 80
The invincible day 92
Forgery 106
The dead zone 116
Hell's bell 128
When the party ends 140
Beyond commitment 150

why

Auschwitz survivor Primo Levi told of an incident in the concentration camp. A guard was abusing a prisoner and Levi approached to ask why he was doing that. Enraged, the guard knocked Levi to the ground and screamed, "Hier ist kiene warum!"

Translated, this means, "There is no 'why' here!"

How often have we struggled with the same thing? There are no "whys" to the questions that need answers—to the things that happen either to us or our loved ones. What about the millions of others—in print, on TV or online—at whose wretched fates we shake our heads, then return to whatever we were doing? The unfairness of their fate chokes us into silence, and their non-answers remain stuck in our throats. All we can do is gasp at the horror of their situations.

Thousands of years ago, the historian Herodotus told of the Gatae people and their interesting yet depressingly rational custom. After a birth, the family would sit around the child and mourn "at the thought of all the suffering the infant must endure now that it has entered the world." In their laments for the newborn, they went through "the whole catalogue of human sorrows" that the person would face. In contrast, their funerals were filled with "merriment and rejoicing," because the deceased has escaped all the woes of life.

As strange as it sounds, there is a certain, almost-irrefutable logic in this Getae custom. Maybe that's why babies cry at birth—something unspoken, something hidden, warns them about what will be. Famine, natural disasters, war, pollution, poverty, disease and crime are just part of the "catalogue of human sorrows."

"History," wrote Irishman James Joyce, "is a nightmare from which I am trying to awake." But what do we face when we wake from history? Do we face the present, which is no great shakes, or the future, which will likely be worse than what preceded it?

Look at the world today: natural disasters, one after another, with increasing frequency; man-made environmental hazards (which are only getting worse); and a globalised economy where the tiniest convulsion in one area can cause hardship and financial chaos everywhere else. Whether we like it or not—and we mostly don't—these things are completely out of our control and affect each one of us. Daily news headlines, scientific reports and economic forecasts reverberate with the questions, "What's going on?" "Who is in control?" and "Where's it all headed?"

In his novel *The Unbearable Lightness of Being*, Czech author Milan Kundera struggled with the seeming meaninglessness of our suffering. Here and then gone forever, human life "is like a shadow, without weight, dead in advance, and whether it was horrible, beautiful or sublime, its horror, sublimity and beauty mean nothing. We need to take no more note of it than of a war between two African kingdoms in the 14th century, a war that altered nothing in the destiny of the world, even if a hundred thousand blacks perished in excruciating torment."

The real struggles come to us now, with ourselves, our own personal stories and tragedies—not with 14th-century African wars. Again, we can do nothing but choke on the non-answers.

An atheist writer told the story of his infant's death from a brain tumour. "My baby! My baby! My baby!" he wailed as the child died in the hospital before their eyes. As the infant received intensive care, one of the doctors kept telling him and his wife "to hang in there." To which he would respond, "There is no other place to hang."

But if there are no "whys" in this life, what's the purpose of "hanging in there"—here or anywhere? Similar thoughts no doubt inspired the famous words of Frenchman Albert Camus, who wrote: "There is but one truly serious philosophical problem and that is suicide. Judging whether life is or is not worth living amounts to answering the fundamental question of philosophy."

Though extreme—and Camus no doubt meant it that way—the question is valid. Is life worth living to begin with, filled with apparent sorrow, suffering, and emptiness of purpose and meaning?

Most of us would answer "Yes." Even if we're not sure of our argument, we are sure that there must be some logical reason.

There are hard issues to think about—we all struggle with them. But are there no good answers out there? Are unanswerable questions about who we are, why we are, what is the purpose of our lives, what does death mean and what is our ultimate fate all we have to look forward to?

The answer depends on the truth about reality, the existence of the world and our place in it. Though coming in various forms, there are two overarching views that dominate human understanding of the big questions regarding existence as a whole and our seemingly insignificant places in it.

So common in the secular world today, the first view was succinctly expressed by physicist Steven Weinberg. In an oft-quoted sentence from his book *The First Three Minutes*, he wrote: "The more the universe seems comprehensible, the more it also seems pointless." When this statement caused a furor, he restated it, saying that he didn't mean that science taught the universe was pointless but simply that "the universe itself suggests no point." Perhaps the classic response to Weinberg, one that catches the essence of this secular world view, was by Harvard astronomer Margaret Geller, who said, "Why should it [the universe] have a point? What point? It's just a physical system, what point is there? I've always been puzzled by that statement."

Of course, if the universe is "just a physical system," then each one of us, individually, is also "just a physical system." If the big, enduring universe is pointless and meaningless, what does that say about the tiny fleeting specks known as humanity? It says that there is no "why" here: that we are the chance creations of a chance universe. It would mean that nothing planned us, nothing saw us coming and nothing bestows meaning on us. Trying to find purpose amid a purposeless universe is logically impossible—it just isn't there.

Though arguing that the universe itself is pointless, Weinberg countered that we can, nevertheless, "invent a point for our lives, including trying to understand the universe."

But why study the pointless—what's to understand? How is that supposed to give us purpose? Trying to "invent a point for our lives" by seeking to understand a pointless universe is another futile endeavour that makes life seem so meaningless to begin with.

The New Yorker magazine published an article that began with the author talking about an atheist friend. This "philosopher" told him that she sometimes wakes in the middle of the night, stressing over a series of big questions: "How can it be that this world is the result of an accidental big bang? How could there be no design, no metaphysical purpose? Can it be that every life—beginning with my own, my husband's, my child's—is cosmically irrelevant?"

If her atheist view of the universe is correct, then yes—it can be. By taking her premises to their logical conclusions, she was confronted with the fact that her life—and all human life—was "cosmically irrelevant." The atheistic evolutionary model offers no other answers to our questions.

And, yet, how she framed the questions revealed her discomfort and dissatisfaction with this answer. She expressed what many feel—that something's radically inadequate with the idea that our lives are purposeless, pointless and meaningless. Yet what else could our lives be in a universe that, itself, is purposeless, pointless and meaningless?

Something, both in our hearts and in our heads, says this just can't be right. The atheistic evolutionary model, in which we are all cosmic accidents, doesn't seem to fit the reality we face every day. It does not fit the world we live in, or the dreams and aspirations we hold for ourselves. It isn't just wishful thinking—it's a logical conclusion to draw from the act of simply being human and living lives filled with purpose from their conception onward.

This leads directly to the second of the two overarching views of reality: the idea of God, especially as presented in the Judeo-Christian scriptures. The Bible gives us a radically different perspective on the things we confront in this world—good and evil, justice and injustice.

And more than anything else, the biblical view offers us a hope for something beyond today. It offers hope beyond what is purely material, beyond this world, and beyond despair, fear and helplessness. Perhaps that's why one of Fyodor Dostoyevsky's characters, in his novel *The Possessed*, said, "Man has done nothing but invent God so as to go on living, and not kill himself."

However, this book argues not that man invented God but that God "invented" or created humankind for a reason. The sense of purpose we have for our lives isn't a delusion—it's a direct result of who and what we are. We are beings created by a loving God who gives our lives dignity, purpose and meaning beyond what's found in science alone.

According to science's view, understanding the laws of physics means we understand all there is to know about ourselves. In the words of physicist Stephen Hawking, we will even know "the mind of God." Then again, others are not convinced that such a view has the answers we seek and need.

"When and if we have found and understood the completely irreducible laws of physics," wrote physicist Frank Wilczek, "we certainly shall not thereby know the mind of God (Hawking to the contrary). We will not even get much help in understanding the mind of slugs, which is about the current frontier of neuroscience."

The biblical world view takes us where the atheistic view can't. This is because the biblical world view is broader than the atheistic one. Of course, the biblical view encompasses the physical world and the laws in it, just as the atheistic view does. But it also takes us beyond these laws— beyond what they can teach us, and beyond what today's science tells us or could ever tell us. To some degree, it truly takes us into the mind of God. It shows us that God loves us, cares for us and has our best interests at heart. In a world overrun with evil, God's love is true—no matter how hard this great and comforting truth is to understand.

Both perspectives—the atheistic and the biblical—offer explanations for why our world is so filled with pain, suffering, evil, violence, climate change, globalism and natural disasters. In the first view, these things are merely part of what it means to live in a world created by accident. If this is the case, the universe has no intentions or purpose for us—it is a universe that doesn't care about us or our hopes, dreams and goals. Such a universe offers us nothing but the prospect of eternal annihilation in a cold, dead cosmos—a rather inglorious end for beings that, according to the evolutionary model, are advancing.

In the Christian world view, we are in the midst of a literal cosmic conflict between good and evil. What we see in our world—the pain, suffering and violence—are the results of humans having turned away from God and the moral order He originally created.

But as we have mentioned, the greatest difference—the difference that makes all the difference—is that the biblical world view offers us hope. It gives us the promise of something beyond today and beyond what this world could ever offer.

The scientific world says that we began by chance and our end will also be by chance. If humankind doesn't nuke itself or destroy the planet with pollution, the sun will eventually blow up. Either that or the universe will crash in on itself, and we and every memory of us are destined for eternal oblivion.

The Bible perspective presents a vastly different ending. The credits scrolling down at the end of the story aren't "Cosmic Heat Death," the "Big Crunch" or "Nuclear Winter." Instead, they speak of hope, restoration and re-creation.

Each one of us has a story to tell but our stories can only be told in the context of the bigger picture. This bigger picture greatly determines the meaning of all that unfolds within it, including our stories. One view sets our lives in the background of a godless, purposeless creation, which philosopher Thomas Nagel said presents us with "no reason to believe that anything matters." If nothing matters, our lives and all the suffering, turmoil and trials that come with them do not matter. If this is the case, why should things like global warming, economic chaos, natural disasters, crime and exploitation bother us at all? In the scheme of such a cosmos, our personal stories don't matter either.

In stark contrast, the biblical view teaches that our lives unfold against the background of a universe created by a loving God. He has infused it with a purpose, meaning and hope that screams out at us—even if we can't put our fingers on it. Even if we can't explain it, real yearnings tickle and nudge our hearts. This view offers us a context to better understand our own yearnings and lives, as well as the world in which they unfold. It also tells us why the world is as it is and where it—and we—are ultimately going.

This book, then, attempts to show that contrary to popular opinion—albeit affirmed by laboratory experiments and the smartest scientific pronouncements—there is a "why" here.

Read on and discover what we believe that "why" is—and the hope it offers us. Humanity has hope for something beyond today and something so much better, too.

*what's your **story?***

Paranoid people—it has been said—have enemies, too. The former ruler of Iraq, Saddam Hussein, is a great example.

While he ran the Arab nation with an iron fist from 1979 to 2003, he lived in constant fear. When Saddam arrived at one of his luxurious palaces scattered around the oil-rich nation, it was usually late at night. His food was shipped in secretly and special chefs were allowed to prepare the meals only after every package, bottle and container had been x-rayed. Condemned prisoners from one of Saddam's jails were then used to test the food. After they ate, their blood was checked for any sign of poison or radioactivity. If all of the blood work came back clear, the testers were led out into the courtyard and shot. The sounds of the gunfire all but said to Saddam, *"Bon appétit."*

While most of us don't have to live with this kind of fear, the world is a scary place at times. There are so many forces at play that we can't control. There are things happening around us that our senses totally miss.

Next time you're in a room by yourself, turn off anything that makes a noise. Stay there quietly and just listen. You should hear no sounds—nothing except perhaps your own breathing. The only problem is your senses have taken you for a ride! Unless you're somewhere deep in the Outback or the Arctic, the room is filled with thousands and thousands—perhaps millions—of phone calls, radio broadcasts and TV programs. All of them are as real as your own thoughts or breathing, yet your senses—in this case, your ears—have left you clueless.

And it isn't just your ears fooling you.

Currently, the earth is spinning at about 1600 kilometres per hour (1000 miles per hour) on its axis while circling the sun at 48,280 kilometres per hour (about 30,000 miles per hour). Meanwhile, the sun is orbiting the centre of our galaxy at 780,500 kilometres per hour (about 480,000 miles per hour) and our galaxy is careening through space at a face-flattening 1,987,500 kilometres per hour (about 1,240,000 miles per hour). We're moving so fast in so many different directions that if we were on a roller coaster, our stomach would be inside out and bouncing off our nose. I've no doubt our lunch would be all over the lucky souls behind us, too!

Yet our senses tell us we are standing perfectly still. They have left us as clueless about the forces moving us through space as they have about the forces in the air around us. All of them are forces we can't see, feel, taste or sense—we have no control over them.

How can we control them when we can't even *feel* them?

THE SEEN AND UNSEEN

But what about the forces we can sense and feel? These forces greatly affect our lives, yet we have no more control over them than over the speed of the earth through the cosmos. Every day, swirling and whizzing vortices of influence, factors and powers shape our lives without asking our input or opinion. All around us, seen and unseen, these forces often don't even know we're there. Even if they did, they couldn't care less about us. Imagine a driver swerves into your path and life is changed forever. A lover's heart could turn toward another, leaving your life in ruins. Imagine a tumour silently forming in a pancreas and you don't know about it until it's too late. You could be sitting in your office and someone flies a hijacked jet through your window. Imagine relaxing on the beach in Thailand and a tsunami sweeps your family out to sea. And it seems the economy just likes to kick you in the teeth.

Bankers in China, oil magnates in the Middle East, earthquakes at the bottom of the ocean, or bureaucrats in Canberra, Washington or Wellington—any one of these or thousands of other things can turn us inside out and upside down. We have no more influence over them than we do over the course of Mars through the galaxy.

Who hasn't had to stand against forces we were helpless to beat? Who hasn't been affected by something they didn't cause, didn't see coming and couldn't have stopped even if they wanted to? Who hasn't wished they could have their own personal food taster taking the hits for them?

What about the Black Saturday bushfires in Australia or the earthquakes in Christchurch, New Zealand? How many people died? How many were injured? How many lives were radically changed by events that victims didn't cause and couldn't control?

What about the floods we see around the world from time to time? No-one could control the rain that caused the flooding. And again, people's lives changed forever—victims of forces utterly beyond their control.

Yes, there are many forces out there that we have no say over whatsoever. We didn't choose our parents, birthplace, eye colour, upbringing or genes, yet any one of these factors greatly affects us. Together, they make us who and what we are. We had no more choice here than we did in deciding, among the hordes of spermatozoa, which would win that race to make us who we are.

A student in a biology class asked the teacher, "Is there anything I can do to change what my genetic structure has left me?"

"Why, sure," the teacher replied, "just get new grandparents!"

BUTTERFLY EFFECT

Scientists talk about the "Butterfly Effect"—the idea that even the most insignificant events can cause monstrous effects somewhere else. A good example is a butterfly flapping its wings. It's an idea captured by poet Billy Collins, who wrote about how a butterfly in the interior of South America fluttered it wings,

> Thus causing it to rain heavily
> on your wedding day
> several years from now, and spinning you down
> a path to calamity and ruin.

Maybe it's not a butterfly flapping its wings that causes such calamity but in the 21st century, in our era of globalisation, iPhone, Facebook and E*trade, it seems there are more forces beyond our control than ever before that affect our lives and the lives of millions of others.

Look at the economic crash that began in 2008. How is it that a bunch of bad mortgages created in the United States could throw millions of people out of work around the world almost overnight and push millions of others into poverty in almost every corner of the globe?

USA Today claims: "The 77 million Americans in the Baby Boom generation face an economic storm: the Wall Street meltdown trampled their retirement nest eggs more than any other group. After losing jobs during what they thought would be some of their peak earning years, many are struggling to get back into the workforce."

That's 77 million people who were affected by forces outside their control.

Meanwhile, the disparity of wealth continues to grow. It's possible that in hard economic times, the rich aren't getting richer at the rates they used to but the poor are getting poorer faster than ever. The gap between the two is still growing. If you search online for phrases like "the gap between the rich and the poor" or "economic disparity," you'd see numbers that break your heart. Either that or they'd make you steaming mad.

Someone in the West wrote:

> Last week, while in a grocery store, I noticed some bottled water at the beginning of an aisle. I followed the flow, walking past one brand, then another, and another, and on and on, a river of bottles—big bottles, little bottles, blue bottles, green bottles, brown bottles, long and slender bottles, short and squat bottles; glass bottles, plastic bottles, six-packs, 20-packs, bottles with French and Italian names, bottles with water from about every creek and deep spring in America. Down the

entire aisle—one brand after another, one kind after another for every taste, fetish and thirst. I'm talking about water, water for crying out loud.

Tell me this ain't sick. I'm not even thinking about it in the context of the fact that about . . . what?—two billion people around the world drink out [of] the same waters that others defecate in. I'm talking about it in its own context—that of a consumer society so pampered it has created a market for its own designer water. . . . Are we so rich, so spoiled, so opiate in affluence that our shelves have more varieties of water than hospitals in some countries have medicines?

The whole idea of the "global village"—the idea of linking the world together in order to facilitate more freely the flow of goods, services and wealth—was all supposed to be good. This was supposed to bring us closer together, perhaps helping spread the wealth. Maybe we could share some of that bottled water?

If we're in a crowded room and someone is throwing out $100 bills, it's nice to be near them. But if someone is coughing out some exotic flu in that same crowded room, it becomes a whole different story, doesn't it? As America's economy went down, it started bringing everyone else down with it. This isn't what globalisation was supposed to offer us, was it?

JOE JIHADI

For centuries, when some religious fanatic—thinking he had 70 dark-eyed virgins awaiting him in paradise—went on a jihad, he was generally only a threat to himself or his immediate neighbours.

But we're a "global village" now, and though this phrase is supposed to evoke warm fuzzy feelings about the "family of humanity" and "spaceship earth," it now means we can trade death about as quickly as goods and services. This means that Joe Jihadi (or anyone else) has more access to killing folks—anywhere from Melbourne to Manhattan to Montparnasse—than any other time in history.

All of this is thanks to the marvels of science and technology. At the turn of the 20th century, many folks thought science was going to save humanity, and usher in an era of peace, prosperity and happiness hitherto unknown.

WHO BELIEVES THAT NOW?

Science and technology have advanced alright—with smart bombs, biological warfare and nuclear-tipped cruise missiles. Humans have proved incredibly clever when it comes to using science and technology to kill other humans. We're getting better and better at it.

A number of years ago in the United States, police arrested a teenage boy for building a functioning nuclear reactor in his own backyard. He did it to try and earn an Eagle Scout badge for the Boy Scouts! If some high school kid could do that, imagine what a terrorist group could do!

No matter who we are, where we live or how innocuous our life is, science and technology in the 21st century have made it so much easier for strangers to destroy everything we've worked for, dreamed about and loved. Such threats might come from people uttering unintelligible oaths and coming from lands many of us couldn't find on a map, or perhaps from people who look like us from just along our street.

"Our entire much-praised technological progress, and civilisation generally," wrote Albert Einstein, "could be compared to an axe in the hand of a pathological criminal."

He said this in 1917. An "axe" of today is more likely to be a 20-megaton thermonuclear device and rather than a pathological criminal, how about a suicide bomber?

GOOD AND BAD

Then, too, there's global warming—more fruit from the wonders of science. You might think, "Well, this is a force we can control." Maybe that is the case but it's only going to happen if the whole world gets on board. Sure, we can do our part and we should. But I'm sorry to say, riding our bicycles to work one day a week, using compact fluorescent bulbs and putting more air in our tyres isn't going to solve the problem.

There's something wrong with our world, isn't there? You don't have to be some Bible-thumping fanatic with a picket sign telling people the end of the world is coming to see it.

Sure, there's good out there, too. But how does the good compare with the bad? How can we measure one against the other? Maybe your life is going just fine but when you sit down to enjoy a nice meal, don't forget the children starving to death in Africa as you wash down your Eggs Benedict with a decaf mocha soy latte. If you are in an exhilarating romantic relationship, great for you—but don't forget the millions of women forced into prostitution and other forms of sexual slavery, some in Western nations. Maybe you're having a good day and that's great—but how many people, whose day isn't so good, will seriously consider committing suicide, or actually do it, while you're walking around with a big smile?

Someone once described the idea of the balance between the good and evil in the world like this: "The pleasure in this world, it has been said, outweighs the pain; or, at any rate, there is an even balance between the two. If the reader wishes to see shortly whether this statement is true, let him compare the respective feelings of two animals, one of which is engaged in eating the other."

In The Rape of Nanking—an account of the Japanese occupation of the city in the days leading up to World War II—Iris Chang wrote about a Western journalist who found a badly wounded Chinese soldier dying on the footpath, his jaw shot away. The soldier held out his hand, which the journalist grasped. What else could he do?

"I just put a five-dollar bill in his hand," the journalist wrote, "which is utterly useless to him, of course, but anyway, somehow I felt the impulse to do something."

Our works of mercy are important but what use are they against the never-ending tide of pain and suffering? They are but ceremonial and gratuitous gestures, about as fruitful as $5 in the hands of a Chinese soldier dying on a Nanking footpath.

It's not hard to get a sense of futility about life, is it? Who hasn't wondered at times, *What's it all about? What is the purpose of my life? What am I doing here in the first place?*

Bertrand Russell, the famous 20th-century British mathematician, writer, philosopher and social activist, got into a taxi cab in London. Recognising his famous passenger, the driver asked him, "So tell me, Lord Russell—what's it all about?" And this brilliant thinker, who spent his life probing these questions, admitted with regret that he didn't have the vaguest idea. If he didn't know, what hope do the rest of us "lesser minds" have?

And here's the sad thing, too. We in Western nations might not really have a clue regarding what it's all about but at least we have a lot of material things—a lot of relative prosperity to make us happy in our ignorance.

But are we happy and content? With all the things we do have, do we have what we really want?

Who really thinks so?

"Once you make a billion dollars," said media mogul Ted Turner, founder and owner of the ubiquitous CNN, "it's not that big of a deal. . . . I thought bells and whistles would go off. Nothing happened at all. Having great wealth is one of the most disappointing things. It's overrated, I can tell you that. It's not as good as average sex. Average sex is better than being a billionaire."

"Why does man feel so bad in the 20th century?" wrote American novelist Walker Percy. "Why does man feel so bad in the very age when, more than in any other age, he has succeeded in satisfying his needs and making over the world for his own use?"

Why? To some degree, we are the victims of powerful forces we can't control—forces that often write our stories for us in ways we don't like. All the wealth in the world can't stop them either. In fact, sometimes money is the problem itself. Look at Saddam. However rich and powerful he was, being overthrown by an American-led coalition wasn't how he wanted his story to end.

WHO'S WRITING THE SCRIPT?

Life is a story. We often ask someone we've just met, "What's your story?" because we each have one to tell.

What's yours? Is it unfolding as you would like? Or is the script being written by forces and powers out of your control? We're not just talking about natural disasters, economic malaise and other forces like them. There are forces that seem much more personal and local, yet they are just as influential in our lives. Someone once wrote a play about characters who rebel against the script they're in. They discovered that it wasn't so easy to rebel in this way.

French writer Albert Camus wrote about the ideal of rebelling against the injustice in this world. He too realised rebellion was useless, in many ways, because the forces were just too great. I mean, who of us can stop the forces of globalisation that are sweeping the world? Maybe Shakespeare was right when he said that life is a story, a tale "told by an idiot, full of sound and fury, signifying nothing." At times it is easy to think so.

We're all in a large and grand narrative. In the big picture we may be only minor characters, yet we are the stars in our own scenes. Even so—how much control do we have over the script?

Gunther was an infant when his father was killed in the war but as he grew, Gunther became suspicious. His German mother got coy and evasive when Gunther asked about his father so finally, he did a little digging. Gunther discovered that he was a "Lebensborn" baby. "Lebensborn" is German for "Spring of Life" and was used to describe the Nazi plan to breed a master Aryan race. The Nazis chose the most Aryan-looking and racially-pure stock of men and women they could find, and then bred them in special clinics. These racially "pure" children were born and raised in good Aryan homes.

Gunther's father was not killed in battle—he was a Major General in the SS, with a wife and three children. He got Gunther's mother pregnant when she went to one of the Lebensborn clinics, where Gunther was born. Meanwhile, his father—a war criminal—had to flee to Argentina, where he died in 1970.

Worse, Gunther discovered that "Heinrich Himmler was my godfather!"

THE GRAND NARRATIVE

However much we are the main character of our own story, we are also part of a bigger picture—a grand narrative that started long before we were here. It is happening right now and will continue long after we're gone. This is a story of forces more powerful than that of globalisation. These forces are affecting all of our lives right now.

And it's in the context of this grand narrative that this book will ask the following questions:

What is the grand story we're all part of?

How did it start?

How do we understand the forces that have caused so much suffering, violence, economic hardship and environmental damage to our world?

Who are the main characters?

Are there heroes and villains—and, if so, who are they?

What is our role in this story?

Will the story have a happy ending?

We know our own immediate story, at least so far. Why not see the big picture behind it? Why not learn things your senses will never tell you? Why not be open to ideas you might have never heard before—fresh perspectives that could make you view the world in a whole different light?

In the end, even someone as powerful as Saddam Hussein—someone who had so much control over so many people—found himself at the mercy of forces greater than himself. He was hanged by Iraqis on December 30, 2006—a death that was secretly taped on someone's camera phone. If he was so affected by forces beyond his control, even with his paranoid security measure, how much more are we affected—those who haven't ruled a nation and don't have resources available to try to protect ourselves?

No question about it: we're part of a bigger picture, and one that was not of our choosing. What we can choose, though, is what we will do with the roles we've been handed. To some extent, there are still opportunities for each of us to write our own scripts.

the great **controversy**

Many who knew Al had only the nicest things to say about him: he was kind, thoughtful and generous. A typical description went like this: "All I know about Al is that he was extremely kind to me and my family, especially my mother. He just loved my mother to death. Many a time he'd see her and say, 'Hi, Mum, how are ya?' put his arms around her and kiss her, and when he walked away she'd have money in her hand, in her pocket. That's the way he was. In my experience with him there was nothing but kindness."

Others said the same—he loved children, loved to help his friends and loved to help anyone in need. Those who knew him knew they had a loyal friend who would do anything for them—even murder.

So who was this Al everyone talked about so fondly?

He was Al Capone, one of America's most violent and powerful gangsters. The kind, loving and generous Al Capone ran Chicago's most far-reaching mob in the 1920s. At the height of his power, Al Capone controlled most of the city's brothels, bootlegging operations and gambling joints. He did it through intimidation, murder and bribery—he "owned" the police department.

His most notorious crime—though his hold on the police was so strong that he was never arrested for it—has gone down in the annals of crime history. On February 14, 1929, a few members of his mob dressed as police and staged a "bust" of a bootlegging operation in a Chicago garage. They lined seven members of a rival gang face up against a wall. Then these "cops," with a few more of Capone's mobsters, gunned them down in cold blood—an event known as the infamous St Valentine's Day Massacre.

The sad thing in the sordid history of Al Capone is that not long before this crime, Capone wanted out of the mob. He wanted to go straight and lead nothing more than a "normal" life.

A biographer expressed it like this: "So, after much anguished indecision, Capone chose to return to Chicago to seek exoneration and ultimately, to abandon the rackets in which he had made his name and fortune in favour of a legitimate career. To choose legitimacy, then, was to choose life. He would leave the rackets forever."

Unfortunately, however much he struggled between doing what was right and what was wrong, Al Capone went with the wrong. Though caught up in a kind of controversy between good and evil, he did not choose to do right. Regardless of the various acts of "good" he did along the way, he still chose the bad and the evil.

THE DEVIL MADE ME DO IT!

Most of us are not like Al Capone. But who can't relate to that struggle, the inner conflict that rages within at times?

Do I cheat on my taxes? Do I lie to my boss, my spouse or my friend? Should I have a drink or a smoke? Should I sleep with this person?

Who hasn't felt this conflict in their mind, heart and flesh at one time or another?

This battle inside the soul is an ongoing controversy. Irish playwright George Bernard Shaw wrote that "life is a battle with the phantoms of the mind." Yet sometimes, they don't seem like phantoms. They feel like very real powers tugging at our thoughts, hearts and flesh, pulling in one direction or another.

There was a popular American comedian named Flip Wilson, who used to play a female character named Geraldine. In one monologue, she played a pastor's wife who came home to her husband with a new dress. The husband got angry and shouted, "Another dress? Another dress? This is ridiculous! This is the third dress you bought this week."

Geraldine shrieked back at him in this high-pitched, shrill voice, "The devil made me buy this dress! I didn't want to buy no dress. The devil kept bothering me!"

Later, Flip often used the popular line, "The devil made me do it." He got a lot of laughs but if we look at the world and the bad choices people make, it might not be so funny.

It's weird, because we can see this kind of deep divide between "good" and "bad" everywhere—and not just in human beings, either.

A newspaper ran the following advertisement: "How do you deal with an enemy that has no government, no money trail and no qualms about killing women and children?"

Who was this enemy? Was it Al-Qaeda, Islamic Jihad, Hezbollah or the Taliban?

No. The ad then explained: "The enemy is Mother Nature. And on August 29, 2005, in the form of Hurricane Katrina, she killed 1836 people, devastated a land area larger than Great Britain and caused over 100 billion dollars of destruction."

Whether in the form of Hurricane Katrina or a stingray barb to the heart of "Crocodile Hunter" Steve Irwin, whether tornadoes or tumours, whether overflowing river banks or earthquakes, nature itself seems to be involved in this conflict between good and bad. In a single minute, a wonderful beach filled with sun and sand can become a place of death and destruction. Fields lush with grain one year become parched and dry and dead the next.

"Man follows Nature's impulses," wrote an 18th-century French writer, "when he indulges in homicide; it is Nature who advises him, and the man who destroys his fellow is to Nature what are . . . plagues and famine."

For all of its awe-inspiring wonders, nature can be a brutal enemy.

We're so used to it that we take all of these struggles, endless battles and constant controversies—whether on grand scales or within our own guts—for granted. We've gotten to the point where we just accept it as the way things are.

THE BOY SOLDIER

In 2007, publisher Farrar, Straus and Giroux came out with an incredible memoir called *A Long Way Gone: Memoirs of a Boy Soldier* by Ishmael Beah. Ishmael was caught up in a civil war in his native Sierra Leone and this book gives a heart-wrenching account of how this kid—at about 13 years of age—was forced into the army to fight rebels. For the next few years, instead of going to school and playing soccer with his friends, this fun-loving, happy-go-lucky child was doped up, and forced to kill and murder. For him, it became the norm.

"We have been fighting for two years," he wrote, "and killing had become a daily activity. I felt no pity for anyone. My childhood had gone by without my knowing, and it seemed as if my heart had frozen."

But Ishmael was fortunate. At 16, he was rescued by UNICEF and brought to a rehabilitation centre. Here, they attempted to get Ishmael and other child soldiers off drugs and reintegrated back into society. Unfortunately, the folks at UNICEF were trying to help child soldiers from the army as well as child soldiers for the rebels—and they placed them in the same rehabilitation centre!

Ishmael writes, "It hadn't crossed their minds that a change of environment wouldn't immediately make us normal boys; we were dangerous, and brainwashed to kill."

Indeed, some of these rebel child soldiers attacked the children from the other side right there in the compound with bayonets. Ishmael pulled out a smuggled grenade and threw it at them. The military police came running in but the kids knocked them down, took their weapons and began shooting at each other. If these UNICEF people were thinking the situation was, "OK, Billy and Johnny, time for recess now," they quickly learned otherwise.

And this happened because all these kids knew was violence. For them, fighting and killing was how the world—their world—was. It was a way of life and they knew nothing else.

BORN IN PAIN

In a sense, all of us are like those kids. Sure, the conflicts we're used to might not be so violent—but we still find ourselves in the midst of our own personal battles. We struggle between good and evil, right and wrong—we just don't know anything else.

What makes it worse is that the theory of evolution teaches that the survival of the fittest is how we've managed to get where we are today. Evolutionary theory makes conflict and violence the norm for physical reality. We're told it's the method of creation itself and if you're on the losing side, it doesn't sound like much fun.

These struggles can make life seem so harsh, hard and difficult. Who hasn't experienced, at times, how hard and depressing just existing can be?

On the 25th anniversary of John's Lennon's death, *Rolling Stone* magazine ran an article titled, "Lennon Lives Forever"—a curious title for a guy dead at 45. And even if Lennon were to live forever, what kind of life was it?

"You're born in pain," Lennon said, "and pain is what we're in most of the time."

What's this? Could it be that yet another rich, famous, creative, gifted artist lived a miserable, unfulfilled, bitter and depressed life? And if someone who had fame, money, talent and power felt this way about the struggles we face, what about the rest of us? What chance do we have?

PHILIPPE'S WALK

American jurist Oliver Wendell Holmes once said: "We are all soldiers in a great campaign, the details of which are veiled from us." This struggle is real and we, as humans, have been taking a beating in it, too.

The questions we'd like to have answered are:

What is going on with all this?

Why is life a constant battle?

Why do we all seem to find ourselves caught in the middle of one struggle after another, choosing between good and evil, right and wrong?

Many centuries before Christ, the Zoroastrian religion taught that supernatural forces of good and evil were locked in battle. This was a theme picked up in the earlier centuries AD by the Manicheans, who also believed in a supernatural battle between light and darkness. The Bible teaches that there's a great controversy going on between Christ and Satan—manifested as good and evil—and that we are in the centre of it.

Poet T S Eliot wrote:

> The world turns and the world changes
> But one thing does not change.
> In all of my years, one thing does not change;
> The perpetual struggle of Good and Evil.

One doesn't need religion to see the reality of this struggle. German Friedrich Nietzsche—perhaps the world's most famous atheist—wrote: "Let us conclude. The two opposing values 'good and bad,' 'good and evil' have been engaged in a fearful struggle on earth for thousands of years."

We may not be able to clearly articulate it or even clearly understand it but who doesn't sense this struggle? Which of us cannot feel this battle between good and evil, even on a personal level? This tension between right and wrong, good and evil, plays out in our hearts, daily toils, choices and temptations—however fuzzy the issues and forces behind them often appear.

In 2008, a documentary film came out at the Tribeca Film Festival in New York City called *A Man on a Wire*. It was about the few minutes in 1974 when a young Frenchman named Philippe Petit hung a cable between the top of the twin towers of the World Trade Center and did a tightrope walk across it. Though arrested after he completed his magical walk, Philippe was released the same day and instantly became a celebrity. For those few minutes, the world stood still and watched him balance between one side and the other.

At times, do you feel a little like Philippe Petit? Do you feel like you're walking a tightrope, trying to balance? Do you feel like you're trying to keep from going off one side or the other, never knowing which choice will hurl you down one abyss or another?

If someone chooses to drink a beer, it could lead to a lifelong battle with alcoholism. If someone chooses to indulge in a moment of passion, it can upset lives forever. If someone, battling inside about a marriage proposal, says "I do," they could be the worst two words of their life.

We're constantly presented with choices and options, with forces seen and unseen pulling us in various directions. Sometimes it's clearly a choice between right and wrong, while other times the distinction is less clear.

BLACK RAIN

Jasmine's best friend in high school made her swear that if she told her something, Jasmine would keep it a secret. Jasmine swore she would and her friend told her that her stepfather was sexually molesting her.

Jasmine struggled with this knowledge. She had promised not to say anything but how could she keep silent? A great controversy raged inside her and finally, she talked with a teacher. The teacher instantly called social services and the stepfather went to jail. Jasmine's friend railed against this "betrayal."

Years later, the same friend got in touch with Jasmine to thank her. She told her that she had been on the verge of suicide just before her stepfather was finally taken away. Jasmine's choice saved her life.

Of course, our choices don't always turn out so well, do they?

In the book *Black Rain*—based on the account of Hiroshima survivors—Masuji Ibuse wrote about a boy who, after the explosion, was trapped under a burning house. His father was trying to free him, using a log as a lever.

> "Come on, pull your leg out, boy," his father said. But his ankle was held fast by the wood.
>
> By now, the fire was closing in on three sides. His father took one look about him and said, "It's no use. Don't think ill of me—I'm getting out. You won't think ill of me, son?" And flinging the log away, he fled.
>
> The boy shouted, "Dad, help me!" but his father only looked back once before vanishing from his sight.

Talk about a local conflict in the context of a large one. Isn't that what our lives are about? Amazingly enough, the boy was able to free himself and later met up with his father. One can only imagine what that reunion was like.

Yes, we're all—as Oliver Wendell Holmes said—"soldiers in a great campaign." The only problem is that we're all draftees.

There are no volunteers, no deferments, no conscientious objectors and no draft dodgers. We're all in the thick of it, with no exceptions.

Of course, if you're in a war and have to fight, it would be nice to know what you're fighting for. Wouldn't you want to know what the battle was about and what's at stake?

STAR WARS

Thousands of years ago, there was a man who had pretty much everything the world offered. He had money, renown, property and a large, loving family. He was also very devout and recognised as upright and faithful—a good citizen in every way. From any way you look at it, this guy had it made.

And then, it happened.

His property and wealth all vanished in the space of a day. Then, to make it worse, his family was killed—or at least, all of his 10 children.

Just like that, all of them were dead.

Finally, to top it off, his body was covered in painful sores.

After having everything, in a flash this man was reduced to rags. He sat on a pile of rubble and wailed.

Now, however extreme his circumstances, life can be like that. You're going along minding your own business and things seem good, then *kaboom!* Before you know it, everything falls apart.

What's fascinating about this story, however, is that another element comes into play.

(This story, by the way, is from the Bible—the Book of Job. Interestingly enough, many scholars believe it's the oldest book in the Bible, the first one written. This means that right off the bat, the Bible deals with the question of human suffering and pain.)

Before all of this happened to Job, we're given a view of an argument in heaven between God and Satan. Although it starts in another part of the universe, this battle ends up being waged down on earth and poor Job is one of the victims.

According to the Bible, we too are unwilling combatants in a "cosmic" great controversy. It's kind of like George Lucas's *Star Wars*—but real.

Living as we do in the 21st century, aware of all sorts of unseen forces around us—x-rays, radiation and radio waves—it shouldn't be hard to understand that there's a lot of reality out there our senses don't immediately pick up. And, with our understanding of the size and vastness of the cosmos, we certainly shouldn't think the earth is the only place with life.

The Bible teaches that there is life out there. That's not bad for a book written thousands of years ago, especially since more and more scientists are now hedging their bets that life probably does exist in space. We often sense that our lives are part of a larger story. According to the Bible, this story is very large—epic on a scale we can't imagine. It is literally universal and each one of us is part of it.

The struggle, the battles and the conflicts we see around us or raging in us can be best understood in relation to the "big picture"—this cosmic great controversy referred to in the Bible.

Whether we like it or not, in one way or another we are part of this fight.

And because we are in this war, we are involved—we are on one side or the other. It's not that we always consciously, with extreme forethought and deliberation, choose which side we are on. Instead, we are combatants simply by being born as humans on this planet.

In the end, we do have to choose which side we are going to be on, just like Al Capone.

Maybe that's why, years ago, Bob Dylan wrote the song, "Gotta Serve Somebody."

> You may be an ambassador to England or France,
> You may like to gamble, you might like to dance,
> You may be the heavyweight champion of the world,
> You may be a socialite with a long string of pearls
>
> But you're gonna have to serve somebody, yes indeed
> You're gonna have to serve somebody,
> Well, it may be the devil or it may be the Lord
> But you're gonna have to serve somebody.

Dylan was onto something and it's worth checking out. If he's right—and we're all "gonna have to serve somebody"—wouldn't it be nice to find out who, why and where our service will ultimately end?

another day in paradise

It was a soccer game, much like any other soccer game, with two teams, one ball and two goalkeepers. There was nothing extraordinary about it except for one thing: the game was being played by gentile (non-Jewish) Polish prisoners in Auschwitz, the Nazi concentration camp.

One of the goalkeepers went to retrieve the ball. As he bent down, he noticed that a trainload of prisoners—probably Jews—had just arrived on the other side of the fence. He'd seen prisoners standing on the platform many times before, so he grabbed the ball and went back to the game. Play resumed and a little later, he happened to turn and notice the ramp was empty.

In those few minutes—between a few saves, banana kicks and a couple of instep passes—hundreds of people had been taken away to be murdered. And the players, most not even paying attention to the platform alongside them, just continued their game!

However cold and insensitive it may seem, how often are we like those soccer players? As we sit in our comfortable living rooms, home offices, wherever—fretting over everything from a computer software program that has locked up on us (again) to the discovery of our first grey hair—how many people are we failing to notice "standing on the platform" behind us even now?

As we find ourselves frustrated, angered or saddened by a scratch on our car or a pimple on our cheek, how many people will attempt suicide today? How many women are being raped, sexually abused or forced into prostitution while we're primping before the mirror?

As we go about our day—busy with this, busy with that, laughing in the office, joking with friends at dinner—how many people are rotting in jail? How many others are being tortured? How many people are living in refugee camps, or dying of cancer or even diarrhoea (yes, children still die of diarrhoea)?

The reason we are like those soccer players at Auschwitz is because that's the world we've created—a world where we just go along, doing our own thing while terrible evil unfolds around us.

KILLING FOR A FEW BEERS

Of course, thinking about the world's evil bothers us and we try to do our little part here and there to help. But no matter what we do or how good our intentions are, things often go from worse to disastrous.

In Philip Caputo's memoir, *A Rumor of War,* he writes of life as a marine officer during the Vietnam conflict. He also wrote of the idealism of the time, responding to John F Kennedy's famous phrase, "Ask not what your country can do for you, ask what you can do for your country."

Caputo thought he could do something for his country by serving in Vietnam. He wrote: "In the patriotic fervour of the Kennedy years, we asked, 'What can we do for the country?' and the country answered, 'Kill [Viet Cong].'"

Things got crazy, violent and insane. The senseless wholesale slaughter got so out of hand that, at one point, the officers came up with a new strategy. "From now on," Caputo wrote, "any marine in the company who killed a confirmed Viet Cong would be given an extra beer ration and the time to drink it. Because our men were so exhausted, we knew the promise of time off would be as great an inducement as the extra ration of beer. So we went along with the captain's policy, without reflecting on its moral implications. That is the level to which we sunk from the lofty idealism of a year before. We were going to kill people for a few cans of beer and the time to drink them."

Doing evil seems so natural, prevalent and easy. Napoleon once boasted that he could make men die in battle for a little piece of ribbon—and kill for it as well.

Lest we forget, here are a few grim statistics of the violence, death and carnage of the past century. This is during a time when human beings were supposedly more enlightened and in control of nature than all previous generations.

The flu epidemic of 1981 killed 21 million people. Stalin starved 7 million Ukrainians to death. World War II took about 50 million lives. Pol Pot killed 1 million Cambodians and Mao killed 30 times that many Chinese. Maybe it was 40 times as many Chinese—it's hard to be sure.

Either way, a million deaths here, a million deaths there and soon we're starting to talk real tragedy. One writer said that in trying to nail down the precise number of deliberate murder victims in the 20th century, historians simply "agree to split the difference or to round off the victim count to the nearest ten million."

With so many deaths, it's easy to see them as mere numbers. We forget that each was an individual with his or her own hopes, dreams, passions, loves and fears—just like us.

In his own macabre way, Stalin was onto something when he said, "A single death is a tragedy, a million deaths is a statistic."

HURTING THE ONES WE LOVE

As we know, evil, suffering and pain don't always come via war, genocide or disease. Sometimes just the things we do to each other—to the ones we supposedly love—can be tragic and full of consequences.

Who among us hasn't experienced how painful and difficult we can make life for those closest to us—those we love the most, who love us more than anything?

Many remember the fairytale wedding of Diana Spencer to Charles Philip Arthur George, the Prince of Wales. Yet within just a few years, the story of Charles and Diana turned into just another unhappy marriage.

But there's one element of this story that's particularly poignant. Diana Spencer came from a broken home herself. Her mother divorced her father when Diana was very young. Tina Brown in *The Diana Chronicles* describes how her mother packed up to leave the family and said to the little girl on her way out the door, "I will be back very soon!"

"Very soon" turned out to be never—and this event affected Diana for the rest of her short and fairly miserable life. According to Tina Brown, 17-year-old Diana met Prince Charles and told her friends she was going to marry him. Her friends were surprised she could be so sure and asked her how she knew.

"Because," Diana responded, "he's the only man on the planet who is not allowed to divorce me."

We don't need wars, sickness and mass murder to see pain, suffering and evil in this world. We all have stories just like this of pain, suffering, rejection and flat-out evil.

BLIND, PITILESS INDIFFERENCE

Which leads to the question: why all this pain, suffering and evil?

Why does our world have to be so bad that, as one ancient poet truthfully put it, the only thing better than dying young is never to have been born in the first place?

The question of evil—and the origin of evil—is a hard question for those who believe in the God of the Bible. He is described in its pages as a loving, caring and all-powerful God. Of course, atheists are also appalled at the evil in the world but it doesn't present them with the same philosophical dilemma. For them, evil is simply what happens in a world that arose purely by chance.

One of the world's most famous atheists, Richard Dawkins, wrote about a bus that crashed with a load of Roman Catholic children. Though it was a terrible, painful loss of life, for him the answer was easy: "In a universe of blind physical forces and genetic replication, some people are going to get hurt, other people are going to get lucky, and you won't find any rhyme or reason in it, nor any justice. The universe we observe has precisely the properties we should expect if there is, at bottom, no design, no purpose, no evil and no good, nothing but blind, pitiless indifference."

Most people, though, find this answer unsatisfying on a number of levels.

Perhaps the most intuitive, basic level is that most of us find it hard to believe our lives have no purpose. It is hard to entertain the thought that we are products of pure blind chance and nothing more. We see purpose all around us—things are created to function and achieve certain ends and purposes. It seems so obvious that it almost doesn't need to be stated. Yet, according to Dawkins, there's no purpose to anything at all.

Maybe he can look at the world and say there's "no evil and no good, nothing but blind, pitiless indifference" but most of us consider "blind, pitiless indifference" in the face of things like war, disease and torture as evil in itself.

When gunpowder was first invented, it was believed it would bring an end to war. Because of the carnage it could cause, people thought humans wouldn't dare use it to wage war. Unfortunately, they were wrong.

Most of us would agree that there's evil in this world. But once we have this point firmly established, the big question is, *OK, so where did it come from?*

THE INVASION OF THE BODY SNATCHERS

It's kind of ironic but Dawkins gave us a hint when he talked about "the universe we observe." The universe of today looks a lot different to the one the ancients gazed on. Centuries ago, people had a limited view of the size of the cosmos, some thinking the stars in the sky were only a few thousand miles away.

Not that long ago, many believed our Milky Way galaxy was the extent of the universe. Today, we know better and our minds are staggered by the immensity of the known universe. We can't seem to grasp just how large it is.

Given what we have been learning in the past century about the vastness of the universe and the number of stars and galaxies out there, more and more people think we're not alone. The sheer size of the universe makes it likely that there is more life out there.

Astrobiology is the branch of science devoted to the study of cosmic life. NASA has its own Astrobiology Institute, and its website reads: "Astro-biology is devoted to the study of the origins, evolution, distribution and future of life in the universe. . . . Does life exist on worlds other than Earth? How could terrestrial life potentially survive and adapt beyond our home planet?"

Billions and billions of galaxies exist, each with billions and billions of stars. Planets have already been discovered around a few of these stars and yet, we still think we're alone. Apparently, NASA doesn't and neither does Hollywood. With everything from Invasion of *the Body Snatchers, ET, Close Encounters of the Third Kind, The Matrix, District Nine, Alien and Cocoon, Men in Black, Star Wars, Star Trek, Starship Troopers,* and dozens and dozens of others, Hollywood isn't closed to the idea of life in other parts of the universe.

Again, considering the size of the universe, it's hard to see how there couldn't be other life out there.

THE BIBLE AND COSMOLOGY

Interestingly enough, while scientists and astronomers point fancy telescopes at the sky and hope to retrieve an intelligent peep or mutter from the heavens, the Bible talks about the existence of extraterrestrial life. Scripture has given us some fascinating insights into what this life is like and makes clear what science suspects: earth isn't the only place in creation with intelligent life.

The Bible not only talks about life existing in other parts of the cosmos but also makes it clear that this life interacts with humanity on earth. More so, it depicts some of this life as hostile to us.

Consider this story from the Bible: "And war broke out in heaven: Michael and his angels fought with the dragon; and the dragon and his angels fought, but they did not prevail, nor was a place found for them in heaven any longer. So the great dragon was cast out, that serpent of old, called the Devil and Satan, who deceives the whole world; he was cast to the earth, and his angels were cast out with him" (Revelation 12:7–9).

It's pretty heavy stuff, talking about warfare in another place in the universe. During this war, a being called the devil not only lost the battle but he and his angels—those who were on his side in this cosmic conflict—were cast down to earth.

It's the great controversy scenario we looked at in the previous chapter. According to the Bible, it's a literal battle now being fought in the lives of human beings here on earth.

Today, many laugh off this idea as mere superstition. For them, the world and the universe is understood purely in scientific terms. Many believe that if it can't be explained by science, it just isn't real.

However, the Bible gives us a view of reality that is not hemmed in by the narrow constraints of science. While the Bible doesn't deny the physical processes of science, it doesn't limit reality to those processes either. Instead, it points to a God and reality that goes beyond what test tubes and mathematical equations could ever tell us.

The Bible presents a broader view of reality and tells us about beings called angels. Though these beings first existed in another part of the cosmos, now they are here. Some are friendly, others are hostile and all are involved in a battle—a great controversy between good and evil that is being fought among, in and through us.

A royal butler reported that Queen Elizabeth once said "there are dark forces at work of which we know nothing." If she really did say so, Elizabeth was a perceptive queen indeed.

Who hasn't felt or sensed something of the "dark forces" in their own experience? There are forces, powers and elements at work around us, influencing us every day. Even if we don't understand how or why, we sense that these forces aren't all sweetness and light.

According to the Bible, these "dark forces" are real. They go a long way toward explaining the horrible situation we face here on earth and the answer is cosmic in scope.

It might be funny when Flip Wilson says the "devil made me do it" but considering the struggles we face and the situation we see in the world today, it's no laughing matter. All over the world, people are struggling with the horrible consequences of evil. I assure you, they're not laughing.

SALIVA-DRIPPING MARTIANS

On October 30, 1938, a radio drama called *War of the Worlds* was played in the United States. Based on H G Wells's 19th-century novel, the drama presented a series of news flashes and bulletins about an invasion of hostile aliens from Mars. It was so well done and realistic that millions thought it was real.

At one point in the broadcast, an actor playing a newscaster in the field described an alien as it emerged from its flying saucer. "Good heavens, something's wriggling out of the shadow like a grey snake," he said. "Now [there]'s another one, and another. They look like tentacles to me. There, I can see the thing's body. It's large as a bear and it glistens like wet leather. But that face. It . . . it's indescribable. I can hardly force myself to keep looking at it. The eyes are black and gleam like a serpent. The mouth is V-shaped, with saliva dripping from its rimless lips that seem to quiver and pulsate. . . . The thing is rising up. The crowd falls back. They've seen enough. This is the most extraordinary experience. I can't find words."

Panicked people headed for the roads, hid in basements and loaded their weapons. Some even wrapped their heads in wet towels to protect themselves from Martian poison gas!

When everything had settled down, an outrage ensued and the story made the front page of the *New York Times:* "Radio Listeners in Panic, Taking War Drama as Fact."

Sophisticated as we are today, most of us wouldn't take a report of Martian creatures with V-shaped mouths and "saliva dripping from . . . rimless lips that seem to quiver and pulsate" seriously. We don't take that drama as fact.

At the same time, considering the size of the universe—and how little we know of it—we don't want to mistake fact for fiction either. If supernatural evil is not just the stuff of movies and science fiction, we want to know it is real. Our own stories are unfolding amid a much larger epic and we need to know what is true and what is not.

While we might not be playing soccer as people are carted off to the gas chamber, we know evil exists. It's usually subtle, which makes it even more insidious. Evil rarely presents itself to us so openly and blatantly, yet we know it's there. We have all seen it and experienced it for ourselves.

Of course, it's one thing to know the problem and another entirely to find the solution. This is "the quest for truth." For most people, the issue isn't "Would you like to know truth?" Instead, the question is, "How *badly* would you like to know, and what would you be willing to give up in order to find out?"

truth **happens**

A young man from a wealthy home—actually three wealthy homes, one in Sydney, one in Tasmania and one in Tahiti—got fed up with life. He decided he was fed up with material things and the overwhelming futility of it all.

There had to be more to life than nice cars, gauche hotels and snooty waiters in expensive restaurants. There had to be more to life than his latest gadgets, smart phones and designer bottles of water. He had the best education, good looks, a girlfriend his friends drooled over and a great future in the family business.

Even so, he struggled to find meaning.

What was the purpose of it all? What was the story being written by his life? Was it even a story he wanted to be in? What epic was unfolding around him and what was his place in it? If he didn't like that place, how could he get out? *Could* he even get out?

Even more troubling was this frightful thought that, even if he could write his own story, he had no idea what to say. How could he when he didn't even know what he wanted? All he knew was the story he was in—no matter how it looked to others—left him feeling cold, dead and empty.

Finally, he decided to find himself and find truth. Much to his parents and friends' dismay, he travelled to Asia. As he wandered and searched, he learned of an old wise man that lived on a secluded mountain. It was said that this man had the answers to life. Hearing this, the young man trudged up the mountain, struggling with exhaustion, backache and sore feet. But none of that mattered if he got some answers. He searched for the truth—he had to know what it was all about.

After cuts, bruises and sore limbs, he reached the mountaintop and saw the holy man sitting cross-legged outside his cave. The seeker fell prostrate before him and said, "I have come a very long way, master. Please, can you tell me the truth about life?"

The holy man looked at him and said, "The truth about life . . . ? Why, the truth about life is . . . a teacup."

"What?" the young man exclaimed. "I came all the way around the world and trekked up this treacherous mountain just so you tell can me the truth of life is a teacup?"

The wise man smiled and shrugged. "OK, so maybe it isn't a teacup."

SUPERTRAMP'S QUESTION

This tale reveals the frustration that people often find when seeking answers, hope, happiness and truth where they're just not found.

Yet how often do we seek truth in the wrong places, through sex, drugs, bar hopping, endless materialism, mindless entertainment, cults, Tarot cards or finger-numbing video games? There's plenty to do—but what good does it do us?

Some folks have argued that we stay busy just to keep our minds off the fact that we're going to die. Maybe that's what poet T S Eliot had in mind when he wrote the famous words: "Distracted from distraction by distraction."

American author David Foster Wallace wrote a giant novel called *Infinite Jest*. It was about a movie so entertaining that anyone who watched it did not want to do anything else. All they wanted to do was watch the movie over and over and over. They wouldn't eat or drink, and were happy to just watch the movie until they died.

In Wallace's story, terrorists wanted to get a copy of the movie and use it as kind of a weapon of mass destruction. They hoped to destroy America by allowing their enemies to entertain themselves to death. The novel was Wallace's commentary on the way people try to cover the meaninglessness in their lives.

He should know, too. On September 12, 2008, his wife left the house to go to her art gallery. While she was gone, Wallace wrote her a two-page note, climbed on a chair and hung himself. He was 46 years old and could no longer hide from the pain.

Remember these lyrics by the British band Supertramp?

> There are times when all the world's asleep,
> The questions run too deep
> For such a simple man.
> Won't you please, please tell me what we've learned
> I know it sounds absurd
> But please tell me who I am.

Interestingly enough, the work was titled, "The Logical Song." A fitting title, it reminds us that it's only logical to want to know who we are and why we are here.

"BUT WHAT'S IT ALL FOR?"

Most people have seen the T-shirts with a drawing of the Milky Way. It has a large arrow pointing to a random spot on it that reads, "You are here." This may tell us *where* we are but not *why* we are here.

In Douglas Adam's *The Hitchhiker's Guide to the Galaxy,* a super computer named Deep Thought was asked the ultimate question about "life, the universe and everything." After 7.5 million years of computing, Deep Thought finally found it. The answer that took so long to calculate was "42."

How can "42" be the meaning of life? You'd almost be better off with the teacup.

A few years ago, *Rolling Stone Magazine* published an article on the 40th anniversary of the breakup of the Beatles. It quoted Paul McCartney, at the height of their success, saying, "We've been the Beatles, which was marvellous . . . but I think generally there was this feeling of 'Yeah, well, it's great to be famous, it's great to be rich—but what's it all for?'"

Interestingly, this quote was made during the Beatles' famous trip to India to study transcendental meditation with Maharishi Mahesh Yogi in 1968. Ringo Starr, Paul McCartney, John Lennon and George Harrison were seeking enlightenment and truth. Unfortunately, their search for truth didn't work out too well.

Starr and his wife skipped out within two weeks because his stomach couldn't take the food.

McCartney left soon after because the place "was too much like school."

Lennon was seeking spiritual renewal to save his failing marriage but when he and Harrison heard rumours that the Maharishi had made sexual advances toward a young woman at the ashram, they both bolted.

Not long after, Lennon's marriage fell apart. He left his wife and child, and moved in with a young Japanese artist named Yoko Ono.

There's no question that people aren't satisfied with life. They eventually discover that fame, money, sex, power, material things and even great personal relationships don't answer some deep-felt need inside. There's this constant quest for something new—something different.

We have many material things but are not really satisfied. No matter what we have or what we strive for, it doesn't seem to answer this ache inside us. Something still nags at us, telling us that our life isn't right and the stories we find ourselves in leave us empty and unsatisfied. So many of us live with an indistinct yet real sense that there's some truth out there we're missing.

Each of us wants to go beyond the doubt and fear that we face. We seek answers, certainty and hope—what some call "the age-old quest for truth."

THE FEAR OF TRUTH

We live in what has been called "the postmodern era"—a time when the notion of "truth" is often denied. An early 20th-century French artist once said something to the effect that he would support anyone saying they were seeking *truth but would kill anyone who said they had found it!*

The whole idea is kind of crazy. Does this mean it's OK to look for truth yet to think you've found it means death? This shows just how fearful some people are of the idea of truth itself.

There's a common notion, known as relativism, which claims that one culture or set of values is as good as any other. It sounds nice—so tolerant and progressive—but no-one *really* believes it, not in real life.

An atheist and a theist were debating over right and wrong, truth and error. The atheist insisted that truth doesn't exist and that one culture's view of morality was just as good as any other one. The theist deadpanned, "Sir, in some cultures people love their neighbours; in others they eat them. Which would you prefer?"

It doesn't matter how open-minded or "culturally correct" you consider yourself to be, you'd have to be a moral moron not to know that some things transcend culture. Some things are more eternal than culture. This "thing" that trumps and transcends culture is what most of us would call "truth."

TRUTH HAPPENS

From the start, it's important to understand that truth exists. We understand that people see things in different ways, and culture and background influences our perspectives. But despite all the fancy and deep philosophical musing of thinkers who define the notion of "truth" as outdated or imperialistic, everyone lives on the assumption that certain truths exist—and that they exist for everyone, too.

Imagine arguing with someone over the reality of climate change and global warming. What could be more ridiculous than hearing the other person say, "Well, global warming is your truth, not mine"? They may as well say, "The earth orbiting the sun is your truth, not mine" or "The idea that poverty exists in Africa is your truth, not mine"? To some, these ideas are on par with "The idea that God exists is your truth, not mine."

If global warming is true, then it's still true regardless of whether someone believes in it or not. If God exists, He still exists whether we believe it or not. We're not talking about one person's preference for Bob Dylan over Madonna, or someone liking McDonald's French Fries more than a box of KFC chicken. We're talking about facts that exist outside of us, regardless of whether we believe them.

Someone once defined truth as "that which still exists even after we stop believing it."

When stretched out on an operating table, you're making the assumption that a certain amount of objective fact and proven truths will be applied to your case. If you didn't believe that, I would almost guarantee that you wouldn't be lying there—at least not voluntarily.

Who says objective truth doesn't exist—or that it doesn't matter?

People might differ on what the truth is or how we come to know it but it should be obvious that there is an objective reality out there—the Truth. Knowing what the truth is makes a big difference in how we live.

In other words, *Truth happens.*

ZETTABYTES, YOTTABYTES AND BRONTOBYTES

But all of this leads to another question. If the truth does exist, how can we even begin to look for it?

Throughout history, people sought to express their ideas, views and understanding of truth through the written word. It's fascinating to look at cuneiform inscriptions, hieroglyphics and other ancient manuscripts and imagine how much time, effort and work it took to write that bit of information down. In the scheme of human history, the printing press is a relatively new invention. The real beauty of writing is that it lasts. The information conveyed exists long after those who wrote it are gone.

But what about us today, living in what has been dubbed "The Information Age"?

Many people remember when their first computer worked in kilobytes. It had thousands of processes taking place in one second—amazing! After that came megabytes—millions of bytes of information per second! It was incomprehensible. Twenty years earlier, you would have needed a computer the size of a living room to do what some of our smart phones do today.

Then one day, we woke up to gigabytes. That's a billion bytes of information happening simultaneously! Processors work in gigabytes and hard drives store that much information. We now have terabytes—but what about petabytes or exabytes, one quintillion bytes or one billion gigabytes of information?

The estimated monthly amount of information on the internet is about 500 exabytes—and growing fast.

In the future, it's not hard to imagine us working in zettabytes, yottabytes and brontobytes!

There's so much information out there available via email, instant messaging, Twitter, Facebook, Google, the radio, TV and the internet—it's growing at speeds we really don't understand. It's not unreasonable to assume that the amount of information created and stored in a single day today could have taken 500 years to create and store in antiquity!

But the question among all this information is, how much truth is out there? Among all those exabytes, how many contain answers to the questions we earnestly seek? We know that information is not the same as truth. You can be an expert—full of information about any number of things—but that doesn't mean you have a modicum of truth.

Let's take note of the Flat-Earth Society homepage. Their Mission Statement reads, in part:

> For decades a small band of self-proclaimed 'enlightened' individuals had been spouting their heretical nonsense that the Earth was in fact round . . . [including] one of their number, who called himself Grigori Efimovich, would later be known to the rest of the world as Christopher Columbus. Using an elaborate setup involving hundreds of mirrors and a few burlap sacks, he was able to create an illusion so convincing that it was actually believed he had sailed around the entire planet and landed in the West Indies.

The mission statement may read as wacky but it is still information.

Have you ever visited websites that claim humans never went to the moon and the Apollo program was a hoax? Once Neil Armstrong—the first man on the moon—punched someone who accused him right to his face of having faked the whole thing!

You can also find information purporting that the Nazis had landed on the moon by 1942. There are websites filled with information about secret weather machines that have done everything from bringing famine to American farms to creating Hurricane Katrina.

We can find information on everything from accusations that Kentucky Fried Chicken makes Black men impotent to the belief that the computer font Wingding has a secret message giving approval to kill Jews.

While there's plenty of information at our fingertips, how much of it can we trust? Where is the truth?

A BOOK ABOUT US

If you were afflicted with cancer and looked up cures on the web, you would find a lot of information. But how much of it would be true? How important would its accuracy be to you?

In the same way, we struggle with our own problems as human beings. We have fears, and a great need and desire for answers. How important is it for us to also get the *right* answers?

For thousands of years, untold millions of people have found their journey toward truth leading them to the Bible. Yes, even after thousands of years, many educated, sophisticated and intelligent people have found truth in the pages of this ancient book.

In one sense, it isn't surprising at all. If you read the Bible, you will discover that the characters are a lot like us. These people lived with many of the same fears, challenges, struggles, hopes and disappointments as we do. They faced the same doubt, sense of failure, shame and guilt that many of us struggle with today.

While the context is different, the Bible stories speak of jealousy, deceit, broken hearts, sickness and the fear of death. Every human emotion, problem or joy is found somehow, someway or somewhere in the Bible.

But here's the *crucial* difference. The Bible—though it deals with all these things—takes us beyond them. It doesn't just leave us with our fear, doubt, pain and sense of meaninglessness.

The grand story of the Bible unfolds against a larger backdrop that we are all part of. It helps us understand the truth about who we are, why we are here and where we are going. The story gives us hope and reasons to believe in that hope. God doesn't just ask us to believe—He gives us reasons to.

THE NUMBERS RACKET

Of course, some people believe that science alone reveals the answers to life's questions. This is a strange belief because if you break it down to its basic parts, much of science is numbers, formulas and equations. That's fine and in many cases, it works very well. The majority of people would want to fly on a plane whose aerodynamics were based on numbers and proven physical formulas, not on some fuzzy mysticism.

But who really believes that the essence of our existence—who we are, what we long for, what we create, what we dream about and what we hope for —can be explained by mathematical formulas? Maths alone can no more explain who we are than an analysis of paint chemistry can explain the beauty of the Mona Lisa.

Instead, we are all part of a bigger story in which we each have our roles. *The* truth is simply that which explains what that story is and what our roles in it should be.

More so, the truth teaches us what our roles could and should be in this epic if we make the right choices. Many believe that these choices are revealed to us in the Bible, the Book that teaches us things we could never figure out on our own.

After all, it took us thousands of years of human history to realise that we are moving around the sun, rather than the other way around. It's obvious that left to ourselves, we are going to miss things and get things wrong!

A book came out in 2008 called *The Monster of Florence: A True Story*. Written by Douglas Preston and Mario Spezi, it tells the saga of a yet-to-be caught serial killer in Italy. In one scene, the writer visited a doctor doing an autopsy. A body was stretched out on the gurney and the doctor had some interesting things to say about the corpse before him:

This one? A brilliant scholar, a distinguished professor in the Accademia della Crusca no less. But, as you can see, tonight yet another disappointment has laid me low; I have just opened the head and what do I find inside? Where is all this wisdom? Boh! Inside it looks just like the Albanian hooker I opened yesterday. Maybe the professor thinks he's better than her! But when I open them up, I find they're equal! And they both have achieved the same destiny: my zinc gurney.

The end of a distinguished professor and an Albanian hooker—the same death that awaits us all one day. After all we go through, all the ups and the downs, the pains and joys, the hopes and dreams—just to end on a zinc gurney somewhere?

It hardly makes sense that after all we've lived through that is the end. In fact, it makes no sense at all.

But many believe there is another answer—another ending. Open the Bible and read it for yourself. Read what it promises and see the hope of a different end to your story.

It has been said that truth is stranger than fiction. In the Bible, you might find that truth is not only stranger than fiction—it's a whole lot *better* as well.

One thing is for sure—the Bible gives a much more satisfactory, reasonable answer than "teacups" or "42."

*where have all the **heroes** gone?*

In our quest for answers, we sometimes look to a person we consider a "hero" who can do what we can't do ourselves. Though we sometimes find such a person, we are usually disappointed.

Or what happens when you find—or *think* you've found—a whole city of heroes?

It has been known as Operation Barbarossa: Nazi Germany's surprise attack on the Soviet Union. It came soon after the infamous Nazi-Soviet Pact, in which the two rivals agreed not to attack each other. Of course, Hitler signed the treaty just to buy time—he planned to invade all along. Once the assault began—one of the largest in military history—Hitler's army was to march to Moscow and destroy the Bolshevik enemy once and for all.

Along the way, the Wehrmacht came to Leningrad, today's St Petersburg. Its capture was going to be, Hitler believed, a rout. Hitler was so confident of capturing Leningrad quickly and easily that he had already printed invitations to the victory celebrations, to be held in Leningrad's Hotel Astoria!

Just one problem: the Nazi juggernaut stalled outside Leningrad. Despite the shelling, the bombing, the vicious assaults and the unbelievable casualties on both sides, the city would not give in. When it became clear that they were not going to overrun it, the Germans decided to surround the city and starve it out instead. The siege began on September 8, 1941, and didn't end until January 27, 1944—872 utterly miserable days later.

Though estimates vary, about one million Leningrad civilians died, mostly from starvation. The two-and-a-half year siege caused what was perhaps the greatest single loss to a modern city.

THE CONCERT

Amid all this carnage, with thousands dying almost daily at the worst part of the siege and mind-numbing horror most of us could not imagine—someone got an idea. The frozen, bombed, starving Leningraders were going to perform a concert!

The story behind the performance was surreal. They had their first practice in the bitter cold of March. The orchestra could play for only 20 minutes because the performers were just too weak from hunger. The conductor, Karl Eliasberg, was so emaciated and feeble that he was driven to the concert hall in a sled, past bodies lying dead and frozen in the street. The hall had no heating and they could barely find enough musicians. Clarinetist Viktor Kozlov said the wind instruments could not be played well because the hungry musicians didn't have enough strength to blow into them properly. One pianist had to place scorching hot bricks on each side of the instrument in order to keep his fingers from going numb.

Despite the incredible odds, the orchestra played on August 9, 1942, at Leningrad's Hotel Astoria—where the Nazis were supposed to have staged their own celebration. The performance was broadcast over the radio throughout the Soviet Union. They played Dmitry Shostakovich's Seventh Symphony, which he had dedicated to the besieged city.

The concert was an amazing propaganda coup. Years later, German tourists visiting the city sought out Karl Eliasberg. They told him they had been part of the besieging army and, as they heard the performance on the radio, they realised they would never take the city. They were right, too.

Throughout the siege and for years afterward, Soviet propaganda was filled with retellings of the incredible valour and heroism of the Leningraders. Story after story was told of the heroic deeds, the courage, the will to fight and the indomitable spirit of the Socialist men and women who heroically held back the fascist beast. To read the stories of Leningrad was to believe it was filled with superhuman people, exuding the bravery, courage and fortitude that only heroes have.

It was a whole city of heroes—or was it?

THE REST OF THE STORY

Over the years—especially after the collapse of the Soviet Union and the opening of previously restricted files—a different picture emerged.

No-one is denying that many acts of heroism and courage were manifested during the siege. But was the city really full of heroes?

While the masses were starving, a small group of leaders were holed up in a secure area. They had all the food, vodka and warmth they could ever need. After the siege ended, a well-fed and even slightly plump woman—part of this privileged socialist class—ventured outside. Frozen bodies were still in the street but she was horrified because, stepping awkwardly on some ice, she broke one of her high heels.

During the worst days of the siege, the hunger was so bad that people were eating anything they could chew and swallow—including books and leather belts. Many would scrape glue off furniture and make it into paste. Pets, such as cats and dogs, had long ago disappeared from the streets. But what the Soviets didn't want people to know was that, after a while, the heroic Leningraders were eating each other.

It wasn't merely carving the flesh off the dead, either, because most of the dead didn't have any flesh to carve. People were being kidnapped and murdered solely for food. Human meat was being sold, all but openly, in market places.

Children were especially valued. It got so bad that parents were afraid to let their children go outside alone. The concern was that gangs were roaming the streets, kidnapping children to butcher like hogs. They were either eating the flesh themselves or selling it. If that were not bad enough, some parents—driven mad by hunger—were even killing and eating their own children.

Others would kill to steal their bread ration cards. People had to hide their cards from their own family members, as they were stealing them from each other. One survivor later wrote: "I watched my mother and father die. I knew perfectly well they were starving. But I wanted their bread more than I wanted them to stay alive. And they knew that. That's what I remember about the blockade: the feeling that you wanted your parents to die because you wanted their bread."

ME AND "MR JONES"

Of course, we—well-fed and often *more* than well-fed—should not stand in judgment on these people. The point is that, as human beings, we look for "heroes"—people with heroic qualities we can admire and seek to emulate ourselves. But how often are we disappointed when our heroes turn out to not be better than the rest of us but, in some cases, worse? Who hasn't been there themselves? We don't need epic stories like the siege of Leningrad to see how often people we might deem "heroes" bitterly and even painfully disappoint us.

There was a little girl—let's call her Sally—who came from a dysfunctional family. Her parents fought miserably, and some of her earliest memories are of fleeing with her mother and two sisters. They went to homeless shelters in order to get away from their abusive father. Eventually, he left, and Sally rarely saw him after. The few times she did see him, she didn't remember him fondly. "Kind of a jerk" was the phrase she used to describe him. Her mother did the best she could but with three kids to support in a low-paying job, it wasn't easy. Then some family friends volunteered to pay for Sally to attend a boarding school. It was quite a distance from their home but she was thrilled to go.

She loved it there and one of her favourite teachers was a maths teacher—Mr Jones, we'll call him. Before long, Mr Jones was more of a father to young Sally than her biological father. Sally struggled with maths and Mr Jones spent many hours helping her. He invited her to his house and she ate with his family. She loved his two little girls, and was invited to many family outings with the Joneses.

Sally said that for the first time in her life, she understood what a "normal" family was like. It was all thanks to Mr Jones, who had such a special interest in her. When the school year ended, Sally's heart sank. She did not want to go back to that horrible state of being called "home." She wanted to stay where she was, near Mr Jones.

Mr Jones arranged for Sally to stay with his family that summer. He even helped her get a job and Sally had never been happier in her life. For her, it was like a dream come true.

Then, one summer day, she was in her room in the Joneses' house. Mrs Jones was out with the girls and wouldn't be back until evening. Mr Jones sat close beside Sally on the bed to talk to her, like he always did, but he had this funny look in his eyes. Sally had noticed it before but hadn't thought much of it.

Now just like that, it was different. Suddenly and unexpectedly, he began touching her—16-year-old Sally—in ways and places he had never touched her before. At first, she resisted him. But then she stopped, frozen in fear and horror. Within 15 minutes, Sally's life was shattered.

That was 10 years ago and today, Sally still isn't the same. Her hero turned out to be her worst villain.

WHERE HAVE ALL THE HEROES GONE?

It's a sad fact of life that people disappoint us. We often look up to someone, for whatever reason, only to be confronted with a side we never imagined possible later.

"No man is a hero," the saying goes, "to his valet de chamber." The one who picks up your dirty underwear, hears your disgusting noises and sees you in private the way no-one else does—you're certainly not going to be a hero to them.

You'd think we would be somewhat immune to the idea of celebrity worship. You'd have to be kind of naïve today to be idolising—*at least for any moral qualities*—rock stars, movie stars or sports stars. Yet there's still this tendency to do just that, only to be disappointed.

After all, who cares how good a performer someone is when you hear stories about what they do in their "private" time? Who wants to follow the sports "hero" who has been helped along with a few illegal steroids? Who trusts the religious leader who turns out to be a porn freak and con man all in one? Somehow, the lustre wears off quickly.

Despite all this, something in us identifies with a hero. Perhaps something in us wants to be a hero or, at least, wants there to be heroes. We need people we can look up to, admire and be inspired by. These people give us answers to the questions we so desperately need answered.

JESUS AS HERO

As stated in the previous chapter, the one place people everywhere have gone looking for these answers is the Bible. And for almost 2000 years, they have looked to one man in the Bible—Jesus Christ.

We're talking about *Jesus Christ* here. Not the Christian church, the crusades or any of today's self-appointed spokespeople for Christianity. We're not talking about anyone or anything else. There's a sad truth to Annie Dillard's lament: "What a pity, that so hard on the heels of Christ come the Christians."

Instead of looking to Christianity, just look to Jesus Christ. He alone is a hero.

Why is Jesus a hero? It isn't just because of the great moral code He espoused and, even more amazingly, lived—though that in itself is a great accomplishment. After all, people espouse all sorts of wonderful moral codes but how many actually live it?

That's part of what ruins so many of our "heroes." They wax eloquently about all sorts of wonderful things they want everyone else to do. It was Machiavelli who once said it wasn't necessary for a prince to be religious, he just had to make everyone else *think* he was.

But Jesus lived it—He didn't just teach people to forgive their enemies, He did it Himself. He prayed for those who hammered nails into His hands and feet as He hung on the cross. "Father," He cried out, "forgive them, for they do not know what they do" (Luke 23:34).

However, Jesus was not a hero just because of the incredible kindness, selflessness, mercy and compassion He manifested in His life. It wasn't just because of the goodness He taught and embodied. It wasn't just the healing of the sick, the raising of the dead, and the hope and promise He gave to those who had nothing.

All of these were heroic and worthy deeds and all were part of why He came to earth.

But what made Jesus a real hero is what He did in the end—at an unbelievable personal cost to Himself—for the human race.

IS THE UNIVERSE FRIENDLY?

We find ourselves in a grand epic. We're part of a much bigger picture with a giant story unfolding around us. Like it or not, we're in the middle of the great controversy between good and evil.

Worse, we're not sure what to do or how to act. For many of us, there's this sense that we're not doing it right and forces more powerful than us—that are not always friendly—are at play. There's little we can do about them and the power they have.

This is why we need the good news about Jesus Christ, our personal hero. Millions believe in Him and with good reasons, too. They believe that Jesus is the Creator of the universe and, in a sense, the owner of the universe. And yet, though He was and is the Creator, He came down, took upon Himself our humanity and became a human being. He bore the full brunt of all the evil in the world Himself to finally end that evil once and for all.

God, the Creator of the Universe, "shrank down" (so to speak) and became a human being. He suffered for all the evil the world has ever known.

The Creator of the universe became part of His own creation as a human being, then took on Himself all the pain, suffering and evil these creatures brought on themselves.

Either this is true or it's a lie.

If it's a lie, Jesus is just another murdered Jew—a black hole into which so much hope, promise and prayer have been poured with little or nothing in return.

But if it's true, what does it mean? Think about the hope, the promise and the potential it presents. Think about how vastly different reality is from how we sense it with our limited senses. Think about how much deeper, more profound and multi-layered it would be!

Someone once asked, "Is the universe friendly?"

It depends on how you see it.

If the common view of origins is correct—that gas clouds formed the earth by chance and life started in shallow pools of water which, after billions of years of cold, heartless evolution, we managed to claw, bite and fight our way to the top of the food chain, only to eventually die and rot forever—then it doesn't seem too friendly. "There is nothing very funny," wrote author Peter Berger, "about finding oneself stranded, alone, in a remote corner of a universe bereft of human meaning—nor about the idea that this fate is the outcome of the mindless massacre that Darwin, rather euphemistically, called natural selection."

On the other hand, the biblical view of how we came to be here is radically different. Not only are we here on purpose but the God who created us also loves us—even died for us—and offers us the promise of eternal life.

This sounds like a much friendlier universe than the first option.

"I want atheism to be true," wrote author Thomas Nagel, "and am made uneasy by the fact that some of the most intelligent and well-informed people I know are religious believers. It isn't just that I don't believe in God and, naturally, hope that I am right in my belief. It's that I hope there is no God! I don't want there to be a God; I don't want the universe to be like that."

How can he say "I don't want the universe to be like that?"

Nagel doesn't want the universe to be any more than what secular thinking says it is. Does this mean he wants it to have no purpose, no planning, no reason, and no end other than the nothingness and meaninglessness from which we first arose? It's hard to understand how meaning could rise out of meaninglessness. It would be like adding up a bunch of negative numbers and thinking you can somehow get beyond zero.

But this is all the secular, atheistic world view offers.

In contrast, the biblical world view offers so much more.

Here is just a smattering of Bible texts that touch on this idea—of Jesus, the Creator, becoming human and taking upon Himself the sin and evil of the whole world.

- "Inasmuch then as the children have partaken of flesh and blood, He [Jesus] Himself likewise shared in the same, that through death He might destroy him who had the power of death, that is, the devil" (Hebrews 2:14).

- "In the beginning was the Word, and the Word was with God, and the Word was God. . . . All things were made through Him, and without Him nothing was made that was made. In Him was life, and the life was the light of men. And the light shines in the darkness, and the darkness did not comprehend it . . . He was in the world, and the world was made through Him, and the world did not know Him" (John 1:1, 3–5, 10).

- "Let this mind be in you which was also in Christ Jesus, who, being in the form of God, did not consider it robbery to be equal with God, but made Himself of no reputation, taking the form of a bondservant, and coming in the likeness of men. And being found in appearance as a man, He humbled Himself and became obedient to the point of death, even the death of the cross" (Philippians 2:5-8).

- "And I heard a loud voice from heaven saying, "Behold, the tabernacle of God is with men, and He will dwell with them, and they shall be His people. God Himself will be with them and be their God. And God will wipe away every tear from their eyes; there shall be no more death, nor sorrow, nor crying. There shall be no more pain, for the former things have passed away" (Revelation 21:3, 4).

The bottom line is that God took on our humanity. In this form, He's known to the world as Jesus Christ. And through Jesus' life, death and resurrection, He has paved the way to give us a way out. Death doesn't have to have the final say in our lives if we accept the sacrifice that Jesus made for us.

So what does the sacrifice of the world's greatest hero mean to us?

A REWRITTEN ENDING

Author Kurt Vonnegut once talked about what a "bummer" life is. If nothing else, he claimed, it always *ends* badly. If we don't die young from sickness or trauma, we die old from sickness or trauma. Meanwhile, we go through life with so much pain, suffering, loss and disappointment and then—young or old, by sickness or trauma—we die.

The stories aren't all that great in and of themselves and, even if they were, the ending is always bad.

Yet the Bible tells us Jesus has given humanity the opportunity for another story—another way to live out this epic we find ourselves in here and now. It's a chance for a radically-different ending to our stories.

The claims made by Jesus and about Him leave us with one of two choices: if Jesus isn't the hero he claims to be, the Bible perpetrates the biggest fraud the world has ever known. On the other hand if, as millions around the world believe—that Jesus is the hero who can change my life today and offers me the hope that He will save the world, eradicate evil and give us eternal life in an entirely new existence—*then what else really matters?*

If we consider these claims and the fact that we are going to die, why not take the time to search out this Jesus and the amazing claims associated with Him?

RESOLUTION?

In 2005, American author Joan Didion wrote a book called *The Year of Magical Thinking*. The memoir tells the story of how, after visiting their terribly-sick daughter in the hospital, Didion came home for dinner with her husband, John. As they sat down to eat together, he collapsed and died in front of her. *The Year of Magical Thinking* tells the story of how she "coped" with his unexpected death and the sickness of her daughter, who died after she finished the book. Didion begins with the words, "Life changes fast. Life changes in an instant. You sit down for dinner and life as you know it ends."

Toward the end of the book, she looks back over the year and writes these powerfully sad lines (even before her daughter died): "The craziness is receding but no clarity is taking its place. I look for resolution and find none."

As things are in this world, there's no resolution—for Didion or anyone else.

That's why we, like millions of others who believe, need a hero like Jesus.

Through Him, we are promised a resolution that just isn't there otherwise.

rescue

At John F Kennedy International Airport during August, 2010, a flight attendant named Steven Slater had had enough. After 20 years on the job, it was time to escape.

But how he chose to do it will go down in the annals of airline history. Slater's story made international news—and no wonder.

The flight had just landed when a passenger, as passengers tend to do, got up to get his baggage from the overhead bin before the seat belt sign had been turned off. Slater told him to remain seated but instead of obeying, the passenger swore at him and continued to get his baggage.

Slater reached the passenger just as the baggage came down, whacking the flight attendant over the head. When Slater asked for an apology, he got more curses.

Disgruntled, Slater then went to the plane's public address system and cursed out the passenger for all to hear. He then loudly declared that 20 years in the airline industry was enough and he was getting out.

"It's been great!" he declared. After grabbing a beer from the beverage cart, he walked over to the service door and pulled a lever. It activated the emergency-evacuation chute, which he then jumped on, making a dramatic exit. Once on the ground, he ran to the employee parking lot, got in his car and left.

Slater decided it was time to get out, so he rescued himself from the plane. The potential jail time for criminal mischief and reckless endangerment is another matter.

TRAPPED

While it may have worked out for Slater, it's easy to get caught up in situations we can't rescue ourselves from. If we are going to escape, we need someone else's help. We definitely can't do it ourselves.

On April 25, 2006, a small earthquake in Beaconsfield, Australia, collapsed a mine. Killing one miner, it left two others trapped hundreds of metres underground for more than two weeks. Fourteen other workers got out in time but these two were trapped in a tiny safety cage. They remained in the cage until rescue workers finally extricated them.

Consider for a minute their utter helplessness as they waited for rescue, completely trapped under tons of rock and dirt. Some of the rock surrounding them was five times harder than concrete. For days, they lived on a single cereal bar. They had to lick water from rocks while they waited for rescue crews with thermal heat sensors to detect and rescue them.

One can only imagine the happiness and relief of those two miners when they saw the faces of those who had come to the rescue.

When the two men were finally brought out of the mine, a church bell in the town not used since the end of World War II rang out. And, waving out the back door of the ambulance to well-wishers on the way to the hospital, one of the miners asked the driver to stop at McDonald's.

The point is simple: without someone to rescue them—help from forces greater than the forces that had trapped them—they were lost and totally helpless. Neither miner had a way to save himself.

This wasn't a case of uttering a few curses, pulling a lever and sliding down a chute to freedom.

While most of us have never been trapped in a mine, we do know how it feels to be at the mercy of forces greater than ourselves.

Do you ever get the sense that things are out of your control? Maybe you need to be rescued yourself. We have talked about this already—this sense of being involved in this great controversy between good and evil, and right and wrong.

We can feel utterly helpless to face what comes at us.

Sure, we make choices that improve our lives and sometimes, our bad choices hurt us. But who hasn't been overwhelmed by things that just happen, completely against their will? Who hasn't, at times, felt the need to be rescued from this world? We know it can be a harsh, cold and uncaring place at times.

THAT WHIFF OF SPOOKINESS

In *The Book of Dead Philosophers*, Simon Critchley writes:

> This book begins from the simple assumption: what defines human life on our corner of the planet at the present time is not just a fear of death, but an overwhelming terror of annihilation. This is a terror both of the inevitability of our demise with its future prospect of pain and possibly meaningless suffering, and the horror of what

lies in the grave other than our body nailed in a box and lowered into the earth to become wormwood.

Maybe Critchley's being overdramatic but then again, maybe he's not. Either way, what does the future ultimately hold for us, if not death?

In Thomas Mann's *The Magic Mountain,* a man named Hans Castorp spends time at a sanitarium in the mountains of Switzerland during the early years of the 20th century. One day, he gets a full body x-ray—something of a novelty back then. As Castorp looked at that x-ray, he saw his certain future. Sooner or later, he knew he would become the skeleton he was looking at—and there was nothing he could do about it.

"Spooky, isn't it?" his doctor said. "Yes, there's no mistaking that whiff of spookiness."

If you want a peek at your future, look at an x-ray of your skeleton.

Foreign Policy is a prestigious journal in the United States dealing with, well, foreign policy. A while back it featured an online article called "The End of the World." Though it was in the context of the media hype about the movie *2012* (released in 2009), the article began like this: "While the apocalypse is pretty unlikely to come in 2012, it does have to happen sooner or later. Here are five possible scenarios for the end of the world."

This wasn't from something kooky or quirky like *The Book of Dead Philosophers*—Foreign Policy is one of the most respected journals in its field.

According to the journal, the five possible doomsday scenarios are:

1. Asteroids

2. Climate disaster

3. Nuclear War

4. Plague

5. The Unknown Unknown (that is, something we haven't yet thought of that could wipe us all out).

You don't have to be a doomsday fanatic to see how scary the world is and we're stuck in the middle of it.

So what's the answer? What can we hope for?

In his novel, *Cat's Cradle*, the late Kurt Vonnegut wrote about a book called *What Can a Thoughtful Man Hope for Mankind on Earth, Given the Experience of the Past Million Years?* The main character is anxious to read it but on opening it, he finds that the whole book consists of one word:

"Nothing."

Is nothing really all mankind has to hope for?

RANSOM

Of course, not everyone has such a pessimistic view of the future of humanity. In the grand epic we are part of—this great controversy between good and evil—there is a hero who comes to the rescue.

As we saw in the last chapter, this hero is Jesus Christ. He has promised to put an end to pain and suffering—to bring an end to this story in which all are "walking wounded." If we're not walking wounded, we're lying wounded—or dead.

Previously, we said that Jesus is the Creator of the universe. He owns it. And yet, though He was—and is—the Creator, He came down to our level and took our humanity on Himself. In order to end evil once and for all, He became a human being and bore in Himself the full brunt of all the evil in the world.

OK, you may be thinking, *That sounds pretty amazing. But, with all due respect, Jesus died 2000 years ago. Look at our world! All the things we want to be rescued from have occurred after His death. Where's this big rescue?*

And that's a fair question. Jesus answers it when, talking about Himself and what He came to this earth to do, He says: "The Son of Man [a name for Jesus] did not come to be served, but to serve, and to give His life a ransom for many" (Matthew 20:28).

Think about the word "ransom." Focus on the idea that God, the Creator, the One who made the universe, gave His life for us as a "ransom." The Creator of the Universe giving Himself as a ransom? It doesn't get much bigger than that.

If this is the case, it means what was ransomed must have been deemed pretty valuable. Let's say kidnappers take a millionaire's child and demand a ransom. The parents agree to pay and not to call the police. They work out elaborate arrangements, secretly and carefully, with just one goal in mind: to get their child back. They don't care how much it costs—they'd give their entire fortune for their child's life.

The parents get the money and leave it just where the kidnappers say to. They have done their end of the bargain. All is set and they are told where to find their child.

But there's just one problem—they don't go and get him!

But that's ridiculous, you are likely thinking. *No-one is going to pay all that ransom, then not come and get what they paid so much for.*

Jesus is in the same situation. He paid a ransom for us with His very life. Why wouldn't He come and rescue us from this world after paying such a price?

Jesus is coming back. It's what's known among Christians as the "Second Coming of Jesus." His first coming was the payment of the "ransom"—Jesus as our hero. Jesus' return is about Him retrieving what cost Him so much—Jesus as our rescuer.

JESUS' RETURN

The Bible has a lot to say about the "rescue." Jesus Himself talks about the Second Coming:

- Let not your heart be troubled; you believe in God, believe also in Me. In My Father's house are many mansions; if it were not so, I would have told you. I go to prepare a place for you. And if I go and prepare a place for you, I will come again and receive you to Myself; that where I am, there you may be also" (John 14:1–3).

- "For as the lightning comes from the east and flashes to the west, so also will the coming of the Son of Man be" (Matthew 24:27).

- "Then the sign of the Son of Man will appear in heaven, ... they will see the Son of Man coming on the clouds of heaven with power and great glory. And He will send His angels with a great sound of a trumpet, and they will gather together His elect from the four winds, from one end of heaven to the other" (Matthew 24:30, 31).

- "For this we say to you by the word of the Lord, that we who are alive and remain until the coming of the Lord will by no means precede those who are asleep. For the Lord Himself will descend from heaven with a shout, with the voice of an archangel, and with the trumpet of God. And the dead in Christ will rise first" (1 Thessalonians 4:15, 16).

What an amazing rescue!

But it gets even better:

> Now I saw a new heaven and a new earth, for the first heaven and the first earth had passed away. Also there was no more sea. Then I, John, saw the holy city, New Jerusalem, coming down out of heaven from God, prepared as a bride adorned for her husband. And I heard a loud voice from heaven saying, 'Behold, the tabernacle of God is with men, and He will dwell with them, and they shall be His people. God Himself will be with them and be their God. And God will wipe away every tear from their eyes; there shall be no more death, nor sorrow, nor crying. There shall be no more pain, for the former things have passed away' (Revelation 21:1-4).

There will be new heavens and a new earth, as the former things have passed away. This is the rescue we long for and look for. It's the rescue we are promised through the heroic work of Jesus.

But Jesus died 2000 years ago. Why are we still here, suffering as we do? When is this great rescue going to happen?

NARROW PERSPECTIVES

In an earlier chapter, we noted that there is a reality far beyond what we can see so we have a limited view of what's really going on.

Right now, a radio station within range of where you sit reading this book is probably playing one of the current pop hits. This means that the song is in the room with you, just like your own breath. Yet no matter how real it is, this aspect of reality is out of your perception without a radio tuned into that station.

Anyone who looks at the Hubble telescope's photographs of the universe has to be amazed by the sheer size and distances of things. The vastness of space boggles our minds. Yet scientists are now saying that the universe we see—the visible universe, with all those galaxies, stars and all the rest that seems incomprehensibly large—might make up about 6 per cent of space.

With just 6 per cent visible to us, the rest is all this supposed dark matter and dark energy.

So, even with all our telescopes and various other devices for viewing the cosmos, we're missing the majority of the big picture. There's so much more to this giant epic than we can ever imagine.

Being human, we are relatively small beings. We have only two eyes that pick up a narrow band of electromagnetic waves. We live a relatively short time on a very small planet, in just one galaxy out of billions in this vast cosmos.

Is it any wonder we have a narrow perspective on things—especially the big cosmic things? We probably have about the same view of the cosmos as, perhaps, a bacterium at the bottom of the sea does of the whole earth.

In this context—how much is out there that we can't see—these texts are worth reviewing:

> And war broke out in heaven: Michael and his angels fought with the dragon; and the dragon and his angels fought, but they did not prevail, nor was a place found for them in heaven any longer. So the great dragon was cast out, that serpent of old, called the Devil and Satan, who deceives the whole world; he was cast to the earth, and his angels were cast out with him. . . . Therefore rejoice, O heavens, and you who dwell in them! Woe to the inhabitants of the earth and the sea! For the devil has come down to you, having great wrath, because he knows that he has a short time (Revelation 12:7–9, 12).

This isn't poetry but a real cosmic battle that has come down to this earth.

It's a story of epic proportions, involving issues bigger than ourselves or even this earth itself. But when the issues in this grand epic are finally resolved, we have the promise of a rescue.

It's the promise of the Second Coming—a promise guaranteed from the first.

The whole purpose of Jesus' first coming was to prepare the way for the second.

When He comes back the second time, it's to get what He paid for.

Why would He pay such a large ransom then not come to get what cost Him so much?

GETTING OFF THE PLANET

French writer Albert Camus struggled with the question of how we are to live as humans in a "campaign" in which, he said, we "are defeated in advance."

His view is understandable but only if you don't believe in God—in what Jesus did for us and in the Second Coming.

But if we have faith in God and trust in these promises, we can live with hope. It is the hope of a future existence where all the things that make life miserable will be gone.

Camus used the word "campaign." Indeed, we are in a "campaign" but in this campaign Jesus—the hero—has already won the decisive battle for us. We're not defeated because His victory is offered to us in full fruition at the Second Coming.

Some people mock this as pie-in-the-sky stuff. But without it, what do we have?

Without a divine, supernatural rescue and help from outside ourselves, what hope is there? What does the future offer other than the grave?

Some people say, "No, we as humans need to save ourselves."

But left to ourselves, we seem more intent on self-destruction than on salvation. Think about the trajectory of human life over the past few centuries. What direction has it been heading in? Look at where we are now and the idea of saving ourselves becomes a sad joke.

In a 2010 interview, cosmologist Stephen Hawking issued a warning to all of us: we need to get off the planet. Earth, he said, is heading for disaster! Unless we get off it, we will face extinction.

"It will be difficult enough to avoid disaster on planet Earth in the next hundred years, let alone the next thousand or million. The human race shouldn't have all its eggs in one basket, or on one planet," he said.

Our only hope, he insisted, is to keep ourselves alive long enough to develop the technology to get to another planet. Talk about pie-in-the-sky stuff. The nearest star, Proxima Centauri, is 4.2 light years away. This means that using current space technology, it would take 50,000 years to get there and find a planet we could colonise.

Our present prospects of getting out of here by ourselves aren't so good. In fact, for us now, our children and our children's children, they seem nil.

Our only hope is rescue. We need Jesus, our Rescuer, to come as promised. He already came once to pay the ransom and according to the Bible, He will come again.

When He does return, we will be just like those two trapped miners—waiting for that first glimpse of the face of our rescuer.

When He comes, He will do for us what we can't do for ourselves.

*proof of **guilt***

Their stories are sadly and eerily similar. Yet, because we are human—because we come with our own specifics, our own details and our own distinctness—each is an exception.

All were children, aged 7 through to 18. Most were in Africa—though it happens on other continents as well. In such countries, the country is often in more conflict with themselves than with their neighbours. And, as in most conflicts in Africa today, the difference between soldiers and civilians has long been blurred.

In many cases, a village was attacked. Children watched as their mothers, fathers, sisters and brothers were shot, burned alive, tortured or hacked to death. The girls, if they survived, were taken away as "sex slaves," or traded in exchange for money or arms.

The young boys who survived were forced into the conflict. In some countries, the rebels "recruited" the child soldiers while in other cases, the governments themselves recruited the young boys. Children were picked up off the streets or taken from villages and "inducted" into service.

Although estimates vary, it is believed that hundreds of thousands of children under the age of 18 have been forced to fight as soldiers—as many as a third of them in Africa. The children are given pornography, weapons, drugs and often little training. Before long, these traumatised, brainwashed and drugged children—instead of being in school, playing soccer and doing what kids usually do—are not only fighting but committing atrocities.

We have already talked about the story of child soldier Ishmael Beah. In his book, he tells of one occasion, he and some other children were to have a contest. But instead of a soccer match or a spelling bee, five prisoners were brought out and placed before the contestants. He narrates this macabre contest:

> We were supposed to slice their throats on the corporal's command. The person whose prisoner died quickest would win the contest. We had our bayonets out and were supposed to look in the faces of the prisoners as we took them out of this world. I had already begun staring at my prisoner. . . . I didn't feel a thing for him, didn't think much about what I was doing. I just waited for the corporal's orders. The prisoner was simply another rebel who was responsible for the death of my family, as I had come to believe. The corporal gave the signal with a pistol shot and I grabbed the man's head and slit his throat in one fluid motion.

He then describes the man's death in gory detail. He mentions that the other prisoners, similarly executed, didn't die as quickly as his did.

"I was declared the winner," he writes. "The boys and the other soldiers who were in the audience clapped as if I had just fulfilled one of life's greatest achievements. I was given the rank of junior lieutenant. . . . We celebrated that day's achievement with more drugs and more war movies."

Beah was just 15 years old when he won this "prize."

THE TRAPS WITHIN

So far we understand that we are part of the great controversy between good and evil. We've seen how easily we can get swept up by forces beyond our control—just like Ishmael.

Of course, you don't have to be a child soldier in Africa to find yourself trapped in situations beyond your control. You may even find that the biggest trap isn't what's outside at all.

It's bad enough being trapped by forces outside yourself but sometimes, those forces are not political, economic or social. They're not from the government, the community or family members but instead, come from within. They dwell somewhere deep inside the crevices, rills and ridges of the mind.

When the traps are inside, escape can seem even more hopeless than when they come from outside.

A good example is guilt. Who hasn't struggled and doesn't struggle with a sense of having done wrong?

For some, it might be nothing more than a little twitch here and there. For others, it's an acid that eats away at their soul. Either way, it comes from within—places that are not always easy to get at. It isn't like the movie *Inception,* where someone can get inside your dreams and put ideas there. If only it were that easy—especially with guilt.

"Everyone is guilty of something," said an author in a recent article in *Newsweek* magazine.

No doubt he's right—Al Capone might not be an Adolph Hitler but you might not be an Al Capone. Either way, who doesn't carry some load of guilt, some realisation that they have done things they know are wrong? Or maybe you have neglected to do what you know is right. You might attempt to rationalise or justify it but the guilt keeps popping up at the most inconvenient times.

Maybe it's constantly there, like a low-intensity buzz. Is it emanating somewhere inside you and just won't go away?

It might not be a ringing in your ears but rather, a ringing in the depths of your conscience—a silent voice that won't go away.

Long after he was rescued by the United Nations, Beah still struggled with the guilt of what he had done. Even though he was just a child with no real choice, the memories haunted him. With the memories came the guilt that would not go away.

Of course, many adult soldiers also suffer from what is known as Post Traumatic Stress Syndrome. It isn't just what these soldiers *have seen* happen that causes it. It isn't just the fear for their personal safety, or the trauma of seeing their comrades killed and maimed. What many struggle with is what they have done in battle themselves.

We're not talking about war criminals here—just men and women doing what's done in war. Often, however justified their actions, the guilt batters and breaks them into pieces. It makes it hard to hold a life together.

Clint Eastwood directed and starred in *Gran Torino* (2008). It's a story about a bigoted and grouchy retired autoworker named Walt, who doesn't seem to like anyone—not even white folks like himself. But toward the end of the movie, this decorated Korean War veteran is struggling with guilt.

In one scene, Walt describes a North Korean soldier as a "scared 15-year-old kid who only wanted to surrender." Walt had shot him dead and all these years later, the guilt was still eating at him.

Sometimes, we find ourselves in some pretty hard places. They may be places of our own making or places we're thrown into. Other times, it's a little of both.

In the end, it doesn't really matter. Just like those miners, we find ourselves trapped and unable to free ourselves.

AND THEN WE DIE, TOO

About 2200 years ago, a Chinese sage named Zhuangzi was about to die. His disciples wanted a lavish burial for him, saying they were afraid birds would eat his corpse if he were not buried.

Zhuangzi responded: "An unburied body will be consumed by crows and eagles but a buried body will be eaten by ants. So you're snatching food from the mouths of crows and eagles and feeding it into the mouths of ants. Why are you showing favour to ants?"

As we struggle through life, with all its ups and downs, there often seems to be more downs. When we finish with life and all of its guilt and remorse, all we face is the prospect of being food either for crows or for ants.

We keep coming back to this motif: forces beyond our control.

We know the past—and all the guilt it brings—is beyond our control.

We know the future—the reality of our mortality, our finitude—is beyond our control as well.

But most of us don't know what life is all about, what we want out of life or how to get what we want out of life even if we knew what it was. Then—even if we do get what we think we want—life turns out not so great anyway.

For decades, the Dutch painter William de Kooning struggled with poverty and rejection. Then, after World War II, he got a break. Suddenly, he had his own shows, his work sold and he was hailed as a great American artist. In response, de Kooning drank himself sick. The more famous he became, the more he drank. He would binge for weeks at a time, until only hospital detoxification could keep him alive long enough to binge again.

But why would he want to do this when he had everything? He got what any artist wants—fame, money and adulation—only to discover that it wasn't enough. Nothing is ever enough to keep us happy.

No wonder, poet Wallace Steven wrote, "These voices crying without knowing for what/ Except to be happy, without knowing how."

THE THEOLOGY OF GEORGE CARLIN

The good news is that we have an "out." We no longer need to be trapped, inwardly or outwardly, because we have an answer.

The answer is "the plan of salvation."

However outmoded or antiquated that phrase might sound, consider our prospects. Maybe right now, things look good. But no matter how good the short term may be at the moment, who knows what tomorrow will bring?

The long-term prospects aren't too promising. We'll either be food for birds or food for ants. You might not even have the option of choosing which.

This is why we need a hero—a rescuer—and a plan to save us.

And that's what we believe Jesus Christ is all about: He is our Hero, Rescuer and Saviour.

But how is this supposed to help us? Some Jew dies on a Roman cross 2000 years ago in a backwater province of the long-gone Roman Empire and His death is supposed to mean something important for us today?

The late George Carlin—the irreverent-foul-mouthed-gross-you-out American comedian—hit on something profoundly true when he said:

> I'm also tired of hearing about innocent victims; this is an outmoded idea. There are no innocent victims. If you're born on this world you're guilty, period . . . end of report, next case. Your birth certificate is proof of guilt.

According to Carlin, our birth certificate is "proof of guilt"? Though George might have meant it to be funny, he hit a crucial truth right on the head:

We are all guilty.

We have all done wrong.

We have all "sinned."

While "sin" sounds like another outdated word, what else do you call the things you do that seriously hurt or cause pain to other people? What else do you call the lies, deceptions and exploitation of others? What about things like anger, jealousy and selfishness? What else do you call the things you have done to satisfy your own wants, desires and needs, regardless of the effect on others?

What do we call what the child soldiers did to civilians who got in their way? What do we call the violence; the stealing; the rape; the child porn; the whole porn industry; the human trafficking; the arms trade; the drug trade; the corporate fraud; and the endless number of other bad things that happen every day around the world?

In this instance, Carlin was right.

Like the rest of us, you have probably said and done things that caused terrible pain and hurt. You have probably made up for it in some cases, while it's way too late in other situations.

What could Beah do to make up for the prisoner's throat he slit? What could a murderer and rapist who confessed at the girl's grave do to make up for what he had done to her?

Then there are our "everyday" failures, which we are all aware of when we pause to reflect on them. Even if we aren't guilty of outrageous crimes, that "little" meanness, dishonesty and carelessness are made up of the same kind of evil. Our unkind thoughts, poor attitudes and the good things we don't do betray our broken nature.

Again, to quote Carlin, "You're guilty."

A DEAD JEW ON A ROMAN CROSS

So what does the death of Jesus on a Roman cross 2000 years ago have to do with us today?

The answer is this: at the cross, Jesus—Creator of the Universe, the one who made the worlds—bore in Himself the punishment of *our* guilt. He bore the legal punishment for each one of us—our shame, our sins, our crimes and our guilt.

Yours, Beah's and all the world's guilt—it all fell on Him.

That's what His death has to do with us, today.

Beah's victims will never be able to forgive him any more than the murderer could be forgiven by the woman he murdered. It's possible that those you have wronged can't forgive you, either. But what the "plan of salvation" promises is that because of what Jesus has done for you, you can have complete forgiveness—and full and complete reconciliation with God.

God is the ultimate Law-giver—the One who set the standard for right and wrong, and good and evil. He is the Creator of all things and the One we ultimately have to answer to. Through Jesus and His sacrifice on your behalf, you can be forgiven all the evil and wrong you have ever done.

It's true that others might not forgive you—the law of the land might not forgive you and you might have trouble forgiving yourself. But before the Creator God, the ultimate Judge of the whole world, you can stand pardoned. You can be cleansed and forgiven all the things that leave you heavy with guilt and remorse.

One of the clearest statements on this topic in the Bible comes from a prophecy written eight centuries before Jesus was born. The prophet Isaiah, talking about Jesus, wrote: "All we like sheep have gone astray; we have turned, every one, to his own way; and the Lord has laid on Him the iniquity of us all" (Isaiah 53:6).

The first part of this text is saying basically what Carlin said: "You're guilty."

The last part, though, is most important. Jesus Christ, the eternal God, has faced the guilt, the iniquity and the punishment that you deserve so you will never have to face it yourself.

This is the essence of Christianity. Jesus paid the penalty for our guilt, our wrong deeds and our sins so we can stand perfect and forgiven before Him.

The Bible says that God loves the world and the people in it. If we love someone and see them suffering or being abused, we are not going to be happy. We are going to be angry and the Bible also talks about the wrath of God. After all, how could a God who loves this world not be angry with what has happened to it?

As we know, the universe is a big place. This means the God who created it must be *very* powerful. Who, then, would want to have Him angry at them, especially because of the bad things they might have done to others?

Christians believe that all of the pain—suffering, evil, sorrow and death—in this world comes from human sin—and that makes God angry. Yet we also believe that God Himself, in the person of Jesus, took all of that anger on Himself. By taking the legal divine punishment for sin upon Himself, Jesus ensured we wouldn't have to face it ourselves.

THE GRACE THING

There is no way that we can make amends before God for the wrong we have done.

It's because we can't do it for ourselves that God has done it for us, through the life and death of Jesus. In the Bible, it's known by one word—the greatest word we'll ever hear and the most important word in all our lives.

That word is "grace."

Grace means underserved, unmerited favour. In the Bible, it's the undeserved, unmerited favour that God gives to all who ask for it—even the most guilty.

Jesus told one particular story that best exemplifies grace. In the story, a father has two sons. One of them says to him, basically, "Give me my share of the inheritance now. I'm outta here! I'm gonna make tracks and party big time."

Surprisingly, the father gives him the money and the kid heads off.

He has a blast, living it up and partying fast and hard. In today's context, he was probably spending it on women and cocaine. But when hard times came, the economy crashed and he had nothing left. He was all but homeless. According to Jesus, he ended up having to—of all things!—get a job.

But if that weren't bad enough, Jesus described it like this: "he went and joined himself to a citizen of that country, and he sent him into his fields to feed swine" (Luke 15:15).

Remember, Jesus was a Jew and He first told his stories to Jews. So a person sent out to feed pigs? For a Jew, that's about as low as you could get. Today, it might be like working with sewerage, draining cesspits or something similarly abhorrent.

The lad gets so desperate, poor and hungry that he wishes he could eat what the pigs are eating. When he can't take it anymore, he decides to swallow his pride and return home to his father.

Here's how Jesus told it:

> But when he came to himself, he said, 'How many of my father's hired servants have bread enough and to spare, and I perish with hunger! I will arise and go to my father, and will say to him, "Father, I have sinned against heaven and before you, and I am no longer worthy to be called your son. Make me like one of your hired servants."
>
> And he arose and came to his father. But when he was still a great way off, his father saw him and had compassion, and ran and fell on his neck and kissed him. And the son said to him, "Father, I have sinned against heaven and in your sight, and am no longer worthy to be called your son."
>
> But the father said to his servants, "Bring out the best robe and put it on him, and put a ring on his hand and sandals on his feet. And bring the fatted calf here and kill it, and let us eat and be merry; for this my son was dead and is alive again; he was lost and is found." And they began to be merry (Luke 15:17-24).

The father could have told his wayward son to go jump in the lake. The son didn't deserve what the father did for him and again, it's an example of Carlin's deep wisdom: "You're guilty."

Instead, the father showed compassion and once the son made the choice to seek forgiveness, he got it—no matter how guilty he was.

This is the point behind the story: It may be that you feel unworthy of forgiveness by God. Well, guess what? You are unworthy. We are all unworthy but that's what grace is all about.

It's giving unworthy people the love, forgiveness and salvation they don't deserve.

In the culture of the story, the son deserved nothing more than a swift kick from his father and, perhaps, the command to go back to his drugs and whores.

Instead, he got a hug, a kiss, a new ring, new clothes and a celebration!

The father didn't put any conditions on the son once he made the choice to come home. The father could have said: OK, you can come back but first you need to do x, y and z. Then you have to pay back some of that money you squandered on your babes and booze.

Instead, he showed "grace"—pure underserved acceptance of his dirty, undeserving son.

If we believe the Creator of the universe paid for our evil and wrong actions at the cross, do we really think we can add to this by doing x, y or z?

What could we possibly add to God hanging on the cross and dying for our evil? It would be like throwing a few cents into Bill Gates's bank account in an attempt to win his favour.

The father accepted the son back purely out of love and grace. He forgave him his sins, took away his guilt and accepted him back as his beloved son.

Regardless of our past and the sleazy, mean, unkind, selfish or careless things we may have done, our guilt can be paid for in the person of Jesus.

Our sins have consequences, most importantly breaking our relationship with God and goodness, as well as hurting others and ourselves. Jesus stepped in to take this punishment on our behalf and to break the cause-and-effect of evil in our lives. That's what God has made available to each of us through the cross and the "plan of salvation."

Maybe the idea isn't so outmoded and outdated after all.

A NEW BEGINNING

We all play what may seem like a small part in this grand epic—but we see so little of this great controversy. If the truth were told, we don't always like our part or what we have done, and don't like the baggage we often carry around because of it.

How often would we like to wipe the slate clean and start over? But it isn't always so easy to do—it isn't easy to get a new start in life.

Having been accused of financial mismanagement, Marcus Schrenker of Indiana wanted to fake his own death. Planning to start over as a new person, he got in his single-engine Piper aircraft and set a flight plan for Florida. While in the air over Alabama, he called in a mayday, saying his "windshield was spider-cracking," the glass had cut his neck, he was "bleeding profusely" and he was "greying out."

Schrenker then set the autopilot for the Gulf of Mexico, hoping the plane would crash in the water and be lost forever. Meanwhile, he parachuted out over a specific location, rushed to a stashed motorcycle and took off for what he thought would be a new life.

Unfortunately for Schrenker, two Navy F-15 pilots reached the plane while it was still in the air. They noticed nothing unusual—except the door on the pilot's side was open and the cockpit was empty.

Worse for his plans for a new life, Schrenker didn't put enough fuel in the plane. Instead of crashing in the deep blue waters of the Gulf of Mexico, it crashed on land. In the wreckage, investigators found a crib-sheet with bullet points such as "windshield is spider-cracking," "bleeding profusely" and "greying out." They also found a campground guidebook with pages for Alabama and Florida missing, as well as his laptop, with a history of internet searches for things like "how to parachute out of an airplane."

Long story short, he was arrested two days later at a campground in Florida and pleaded guilty to a host of crimes.

He got a new life, alright—but not what he hoped for.

Starting over isn't easy, yet how many of us feel like those child soldiers must have felt?

How many desire the chance to escape and change the direction of their life?

How many want to find a new start and take the opportunity to change the story we find ourselves in?

Through the cross, Jesus offers us a way out—a chance to start over for a new beginning. First and foremost, He does it by taking away the burdens of guilt that so many of us carry around.

These are amazing, life-changing claims. It's no wonder that so many people have reached out and made them their own.

signs and **laws**

In February of 1996, three young people in Florida, USA, decided to pull a little prank by taking down a stop sign. Nissa Baillie, Christopher Cole and Thomas Miller just went behind the sign, unscrewed it from the post and threw it on the ground. They thought it would be funny and besides, it would be one less rule to follow.

Within an hour, a trucker slammed into the side of a passenger car due to not seeing any stop sign. The car had three teenagers inside, who had just left a bowling alley.

All of the passengers were 18 years old—all died.

Here's how the *New York Times* described the courtroom scene, when the three faced sentencing:

> "I understand your parents love you as much as these parents loved their children—there are no winners in this case," Judge Bob Mitcham of Hillsborough County Circuit Court told the young woman and two young men who were convicted last month of manslaughter.
>
> The three teenage victims, all 18, were killed after a night of bowling when they were broadsided as they drove through an intersection. The stop sign was found on the roadside near the accident.
>
> Turning to the sobbing families of those killed, Judge Mitcham said: "My heart breaks for you."

Who hasn't been in a car crash or know someone who has been in one because a driver violated one of those pain-in-the-neck burdensome rules, laws or signs?

Rules, laws, signs and regulations are there for a purpose. In many cases, they are there for our own good.

UNWRITTEN LAWS

A tourist was travelling in the Middle East, visiting the Golan Heights along the border of Israel and Syria. It's not the most serene place in the world, to be sure. He got out of his car and went to walk around, stretch his legs, take in the scenery and enjoy the fresh air.

He saw a sign written in half a dozen languages: Hebrew, Arabic, English, French, German and Spanish. In English, it reads, "Caution! Land mines!" The idea is to warn you that walking here is a bad idea because if you do, you might be blown up.

In one sense, you could argue that the warning sign was trampling on his individual freedom because an agency outside himself was placing a restriction on him and his actions. But if you were there in that area, wouldn't you be glad of this restriction?

I can't imagine someone looking at this warning sign—this restriction—and thinking, *How dare the government tell me what to do? I am free. I should have the right to walk where I want to.*

Almost everyone—even those among us who consider themselves "free thinkers," or liberal in moral, political and social views—knows that to live in any kind of civil or sane society, rules and regulations are a necessity. We need at least some laws to tell us what we should or should not do, even if it means placing some restrictions on us and our freedom.

No matter how much of a free thinker you are and how morally liberal you deem yourself, who's going to complain about laws that restrict the sexual freedom of rapists and child molesters?

You might remember the name "Josef Fritzl." In 2008, he made international news when it became public that he held his daughter captive in a cell under his house for 24 years.

During this time, the Austrian man repeatedly raped the young woman, fathering seven children by her. Even worse, half of those children never saw daylight until they were freed. The idea of a father holding his own daughter captive for 24 years, raping her and fathering children by her shocked the world.

One sentiment you didn't hear about this sickening story is: *What gives anyone the right to morally condemn this man's actions? Who are we to impose our moral standards on anyone else? What gives us the right to say our moral codes and dislike of what he did should stand in judgment on Mr Fritzl?*

It's almost as if there's an unwritten universal moral code that says something to the effect of: "A person's personal desire to kill me doesn't supersede my desire to live. A person's desire to force me to have sex with him or her doesn't supersede my desire not to have sex with that person. A person's desire to steal my car doesn't supersede my desire to keep it. A parent's desire to abuse his or her child doesn't supersede the child's desire not to be abused."

Again, what free thinker is going to complain about laws that restrict the economic freedom of people who want to mug them, beat them up, and steal their purse or wallet?

Of course, just because something is a law doesn't make it good. On the contrary, bad laws are passed all the time. Even worse, there can be completely democratic bad laws that are voted in by a majority.

For instance, from the 1880s to the 1960s, many American states enforced segregation through "Jim Crow" laws. All over America, states imposed legal punishments for consorting with members of another race. The most common types of laws forbade intermarriage, and ordered business owners and public institutions to keep blacks and whites separated.

Just a few examples:

- "No person or corporation shall require any white female nurse to nurse in wards or rooms in hospitals, either public or private, in which negro men are placed."

- "All passenger stations in this state operated by any motor transportation company shall have separate waiting rooms or space and separate ticket windows for the white and coloured races."

Even in death, segregation existed between the black and the white citizens.

- "The officer in charge shall not bury, or allow to be buried, any coloured persons upon ground set apart or used for the burial of white persons."

These were legally-binding laws, created democratically by the majority! And yet, who now would say, "Who are we to judge these actions as wrong? Who are we to impose our moral code on others?" Some things are just wrong, regardless of what the culture of the time says.

Let's do what scientists call a "thought experiment."

Let's suppose the Nazis won World War II and took over the whole world. Imagine that Herr Goebbels, the Nazi Minister of Propaganda—that was his official title—was able to convince the whole world that every person with at least one Jewish grandparent needed to be killed, regardless of age or gender. In this scenario, the whole world believes that everyone one-quarter Jewish or more needs to be executed.

Would it, then, be wrong to kill these people? If moral codes are like Cakewalk Jazz or Abstract Expressionism, as purely and solely human creations, on what basis could you argue against such genocide? How could what every human believes to be right really be wrong? If humans decide for themselves what is right and wrong, it means killing those "tainted" by Jewish ancestry would be right. We would have no choice but to accept it as right because humanity, the ultimate source of all morality, deems it so.

And, yet, if you aren't comfortable with that answer—which most of us wouldn't be—it implies that some moral standard transcends human culture, customs, traditions, rules and laws.

"FOR YOUR GOOD"

Putting aside transcendent law, let's go back to the idea of human-made rules, laws and regulations. As we have seen in many cases, they are needed. After all, what parent doesn't have rules restricting what their young children do?

"Don't play with matches," they might say. "Don't play in the street,"

"Don't take any of these pills in my medicine cabinet,"

"Don't go in the pool unsupervised" or

"Don't stick anything in the electric socket."

But why not let the child be free to do what the child wants? A parent can be as much a pain in the neck as a road sign is, yet we know these rules and restrictions are necessary.

The Bible puts an interesting spin on the topic of law.

> And now, Israel, what does the Lord your God require of you, but to fear the Lord your God, to walk in all His ways and to love Him, to serve the Lord your God with all your heart and with all your soul, and to keep the commandments of the Lord and His statutes which I command you today for your good? (Deuteronomy 10:12, 13).

He tells His people to obey Him "for your good."

Interestingly enough, the word for "your" in the Hebrew is in the singular. That is, it is talking about each individual on a personal level. The Lord is telling each one, individually, to obey His commandments for their own personal good. It's a lot like the way a parent tells each individual child, for that child's own wellbeing, not to eat any of the pills in the medicine cabinet. Just like those traffic rules, they're there for the good of those who obey them.

The Bible verse above also mentions the "commandments of the Lord."

The "commandments of the Lord" means the Ten Commandments. Many people think that, while they might have been useful for the folks in antiquity, taking the Ten Commandments seriously in the 21st century could be compared to riding a chariot on the freeway. How are rules written so long ago applicable in this day and age?

Let's try another "thought experiment." This time, envision our world but with the basic principles of the Ten Commandments as the norm. Rather than greed, revenge, immorality, violence and terror being the norm, imagine if the laws about not stealing, not killing, not coveting, not worshipping idols and not committing adultery were uniformly obeyed.

How different would that world be from the one we live in now? Or, better yet, which world would you prefer to live in? Which would you prefer to raise your children in?

Perhaps the Ten Commandments aren't so outdated after all.

A social worker in South Philadelphia tells of a 14-year-old girl, heavy with child, who walked into a health clinic. Tears streaming from her eyes, she says, "I know God forgives my sin, but"—staring down at her swollen belly—"the consequences don't go away as easily."

It would be bad enough if the consequences of our wrongs acts and our disobedience only hurt us. But in most cases, it doesn't work that way.

In his novel *Infinite Jest,* David Foster Wallace tells of a teenage tennis player who kills himself by drinking cyanide in a glass of flavoured milk. Hearing "the thump of the kid keeling over," the father rushes into the kitchen and administers mouth-to-mouth resuscitation.

The only problem is that the dad gets some of the NaCN-laced milk in his mouth and also dies. Mum enters and "sees them both lying there bright blue and stiffening." She gives dad mouth-to-mouth, only to drop dead as well. This unfortunate family has six more kids and, as all are trained in mouth-to-mouth, "by the end of the night the whole family's lying there blue-hued and stiff as posts."

However far-fetched and silly the story may be, it presents a truth that's neither. None of us live in a vacuum—our lives and actions influence others, exponentially and often negatively. As mentioned earlier, scientists describe this as the "Butterfly Effect"—the idea that even insignificant events, such as a butterfly flapping its wings, can have monstrous effects later.

CONSEQUENCES

Look at how violence, crime, pain, suffering, war, greed and devastation cover our world. This is the result of a world in rebellion against the basic principles of the Ten Commandments. If you went back far enough, you would find that the root of so much human misery and suffering is found in violation of God's moral law. This moral law is summarised in the Ten Commandments.

After all, who hasn't been—or doesn't know someone who has been—a victim of someone violating one of the Ten Commandments?

Think about your own story. How many times have you been hurt by someone violating one of those commandments? How many people have you hurt through your violation of them?

Or, as we have all done, how often have we hurt ourselves through violating them?

Ask the wife whose husband cheated on her if she thinks the Ten Commandments—particularly the one about adultery—are outdated.

Ask the children from a broken home, ruined by a parent committing adultery, if this particular thou-shalt-not seems so antiquated and outdated.

Some may remember Dean Shillingsworth, the two-year-old boy whose body was found in a suitcase floating on a lake in Sydney's south west in late 2007. I wonder what young Dean—if he could answer—would say about the Ten Commandments being outdated?

I'm sure the thousands of people who lost their savings in Bernie Madoff's ponzi scheme would disagree that the Ten Commandments are outdated—particularly the one about lying and stealing.

In short, a whole lot of people would be a lot better off now—ourselves included—if more folks were keeping the Ten Commandments.

There was a girl—let's call her "Sue"—who married her childhood sweetheart. Things were great for a number of years but then, as in any marriage, stresses and strains came in. Sue's husband was away a lot and when he was home, he was often tired, aloof and cold. Things looked great on the surface but deep down, she was terribly unhappy.

Then she met George in a grocery store and they exchanged email addresses over something innocent. Before long, one thing led to another and they had an affair.

After awhile, Sue started feeling guilty. She broke it off and, determined to try and make her marriage work, she confessed to her husband. The two of them got counselling and it looked like things were going to be alright.

Even better, she finally got pregnant after years of trying.

The only problem is that she had caught genital herpes from George. The saddest part is how she found out she had the infection. Her baby caught it at birth and died two months later.

To say the commandments of God are outdated is on the same level as saying the law of gravity or the laws of thermodynamics are no longer relevant.

God has given humans His moral law in the Ten Commandments for good reason. If kept, they form a wall of protection—a hedge that helps protect us from the pain and suffering the world brings.

The law isn't there to oppress us and neither are traffic laws. In a sense, the law frees us from the horrible consequences of violating the laws.

LET YOUR CONSCIENCE BE YOUR GUIDE

But can't we kind of figure this out on our own? Surely humans can work out what is right and wrong for themselves?

It may sound like common sense but it isn't always that easy to do. Polish poetess Wislawa Szymborska wrote:

> "How should we live?" someone asked me in a letter.
> I meant to ask him
> the same thing.

We don't always know the right thing to do, and what we do isn't always right or good. Humans have the capacity to rationalise away the most unjust and lurid things.

Maximilien Robespierre was the key voice behind the incredible wave of violence during the French Revolution. Somehow, he completely justified his actions—actions that are looked upon today in horror, even by defenders of the Revolution.

At one point, at the height of the violence, a mob ran to the prisons. They grabbed hundreds of prisoners—many incarcerated on the flimsiest of reasons—and dragged them out of their cells. They then chopped all their heads off right there on the streets. Things got so bad that homeowners complained: all the spilled human blood was fouling the air in their neighbourhoods and causing the price of their houses to fall.

Robespierre rationalised and defended these horrors:

> Amid this general movement, the approach of foreign enemies reawakened the feelings of indignation and vengeance that still smouldered in people's hearts against the traitors.... Before leaving their hearths, their wives and children, the citizens ... wanted to see the punishment of the conspirators that had so often been promised; people rushed to the prisons ...

As they say, the rest is history. It's a pretty gruesome history that horrifies almost everyone today. Yet at the time, it was justified in the hearts, minds, and consciences of many sincere people.

Another perspective comes from 18th-century French writer Jean-Jacques Rousseau: "O conscience! Conscience! Thou divine instinct, thou certain guide of an ignorant and confined, though intelligent and free being—thou infallible judge of good and evil, who makest man to resemble the Deity."

The conscience is hardly infallible. How safe do you think the world would be if the only law out there was the law of individual conscience? Suppose people were free to act any way they wanted as long as they acted in accord with their own conscience?

Perhaps following his own conscience, Rousseau fathered five children with a de facto partner. He then dumped all five children into an orphanage, excusing his actions with the idea that they'd be better off there than amid the deviousness of "high society" in which he liked to hobnob. Later, feeling guilty—his conscience apparently changed—he regretted his actions.

These are the actions of a man who considered his conscience to be the ultimate guide. Consider this: "If there is a God, then He gives us not only life but also consciousness and awareness. If I live my life according to my God-given insights, then I cannot go wrong, and even if I do, I know that I have acted in good faith."

It sounds reasonable and well thought out. Doesn't listening to your inner voice, your heart and soul, make sense? Surely it's right to exercise these "God-given insights" in which you act "in good faith." How could anyone go wrong doing that? The only problem is that Adolph Hitler, to whom the quote belongs, thought the same way.

LORD OF THE FLIES

In light of these thoughts, consider the meaning of this Bible text: "In those days there was no king in Israel; everyone did what was right in his own eyes" (Judges 21:25).

Notice that everyone did what was "right in his own eyes." This means that each person followed his or her own conscience—or heart. Unfortunately, this kind of thinking led to all sorts of horrible practices.

As human beings, we need God's law as a standard for right and wrong. It exists beyond our own view of good and evil. We need something beyond our own perspective—our eyes are often skewed and twisted by subjective and personal forces that blind us to the rightness or wrongness of our actions.

In the 1950s, author William Golding published a novel called *Lord of the Flies*. It was about a group of English children stranded on an island after a plane crash. There were no adults involved—only kids aged 6 to 12. The gist of the story is that the kids become involved in a struggle for power, control and leadership—a struggle that degenerates into strife, violence and murder.

After killing Simon and "Piggy," the story centres on Jack trying to kill Ralph over who will be in control. Eventually, Jack stages a kind of *coup d'état*. Most of the children side with him until only Ralph is left, fleeing for his life. Ralph hides in a forest and Jack orders the boys to burn the forest down, hoping to force Ralph out so he can kill him.

The story ends when a passing English navy vessel, seeing the smoke from this fire, lands on the island and rescues the children before Ralph is murdered. At one point, a British Navy officer sees a child standing on the beach. Knowing nothing about what is going on, the officer describes him as "a little boy" standing before him looking dirty and dishevelled.

This "little boy" is Jack!

What made Golding's book so powerful—and controversial—is that he used children as symbols for human depravity. Interestingly, that's what the Bible has been teaching for millennia about humanity.

The Bible says we are all imperfect beings, with what Christians refer to as "sinful natures." Though this idea comes under a lot of criticism, all you have to do is look around at the world and human history. Look at the past century with its war, violence, greed, murder and crime. The Christian view of human sinfulness shouldn't be so readily and hastily dismissed.

Next look at how the 21st century has started. Do we have the slightest reason to think this century is going to be any better than the previous one? Who do we think is going to cause most of the misery? For the most part, it will be human beings and what they do to each other. It's what poet e e cummings called "manunkind."

God's law is there to be a shield—a protection. In the same way a parent makes rules for their children, so our Father in heaven has made those rules for us, for "your good."

THE HORIZONTAL AND THE VERTICAL

Consider this extract from a horrific Bible story: "And they have built the high places of Tophet, which is in the Valley of the Son of Hinnom, to burn their sons and their daughters in the fire, which I did not command, nor did it come into My heart" (Jeremiah 7:31).

God says the idea of sacrificing children "never entered His heart." This is a poetic way of saying God never intended for humans to do such horrible things. God is a God of love—He loves human beings and wants what's best for us.

That's why He gave us His law, the Ten Commandments. Going back to the analogy of traffic laws and rules or a parent who sets guidelines for their children, it's the same principle.

Over the centuries, people have seen two overarching principles in the Ten Commandments.

The first four deal with what could be called the "vertical"—our relationship to God.

These commandments help us keep our attention focused upward, toward God and the transcendent. They help us realise that He is God, our Creator. We owe Him our greatest allegiance because He is the one in whom, the Bible says, "we live and move and have our being" (Acts 17:28).

These commandments help us remember that someone is always watching. Because Someone knows what we do, what we think and how we act, we will have to answer for what we have done some day.

But we are also assured that there is also Someone with us, who is willing to guide us in making choices and give us power to live better. There's a hope beyond what this world—full of false gods and failed promises—can offer us.

And then there are the last six that deal with the "horizontal"—our relationship to other people: things like murder, lying, stealing and other things that cause so much grief when violated.

Together, these 10 precepts cover all the bases. Someone once asked Jesus what the greatest commandment was. He responded:

> 'You shall love the Lord your God with all your heart, with all your soul, and with all your mind.' This is the first and great commandment. And the second is like it: 'You shall love your neighbor as yourself' (Matthew 22:37–39).

He manages to mention both the vertical—love to God—and the horizontal—love to others.

It's all there for our own good. Imagine a world where love for God and love for others are the ruling paradigm. It's hard to imagine because in our world, love of self comes first and everything else follows. If you get in the way of my self-love, you better watch out!

The Ten Commandments point to something better, nobler and higher. Think about your own life. How much better would it be if you followed these principles?

Now imagine everyone else believed as well and you can get an idea of how good and relevant God's law really is.

the invincible day

Some people are old enough to remember when you had to dial a phone manually—actually putting your finger in the round circle and moving it for each digit —in order to dial a phone number. The numbers 2 or 3 weren't too bad but by the time you got 8, 9 or 0, you had to move your hand around the whole circle! It was very time consuming—it probably took as long as 15 or 20 seconds.

Then, of course, came touch phones that really sped up the process of making a call. But even that wasn't enough so someone invented speed dials. All you have to do to make a call now is hit one button.

Of course, the computer is much faster than it was a few decades ago. The average home computer today works at speeds that a whole room of computers couldn't match 40 years ago. Some can remember being astonished at having a computer that could fly along at a few thousand computations a second. If you think about it, it's pretty amazing.

Then computers were working at a head-buzzing one million computations per second. A million computations per second is a whole megahertz. Some machines were actually working at 33 megahertz—and faster. You have to wonder why, at that speed, they didn't take up wings and fly away. Today, computers that run in megahertz are like 8-track cassette players. The average home computer works in billions of computations per second—gigahertz.

Though as they say, once you buy a new computer and get it home, it's already outdated by the time you open the box. Which is why, in five years, most new software probably won't be able to run on machines that work "only" in gigahertz. The programs would be too slow for the new machines.

Indeed, some computers run in petaflops—a quadrillion operations per second. A quadrillion is one thousand million million—a 10 with 15 zeros after it. Right now, the computers that run at these speeds take up the size of a house, similar to the space a gigahertz computer once covered.

Things just keep getting faster and faster, including us.

Who doesn't get ticked off when a flight is delayed a few hours? That's a few extra hours on a flight that covers thousands of miles—a distance that might have taken weeks 100 years ago. Might be worth thinking about when you find yourself stressing about an extra two hours delay!

As for communication, we can communicate with anyone around the world in an instant. All we have to do is push a button on the phone and in seconds, we can communicate with someone on another continent. Yet, for most of the past 500 or 5000 years, this kind of communication took months.

We take these things for granted, too. Someone once told me about his daughter, born in the mid 1990s, who was astonished that her dad didn't have the internet as a child.

"You didn't have the internet?" she said, utterly aghast. "How did you send mail?"

Have you ever noticed that no matter how fast we move or how quickly we get things done, it's never fast enough?

NEVER CONTENT

In 1899, a Belgian race car driver named Camille Jenatzy built an electric car that went an astounding 65.79 miles per hour (about 105 kilometres per hour). At the time, this was a world record.

Jenatzy named the car, too. He called it "La Jamais Content" which, translated from the French, means "The Never Satisfied."

Even with the fastest car, he was never happy and never satisfied. It says something about the world we live in today.

We have faster trains, faster cars, faster planes, faster mail, faster computers and faster ways of communicating—everything is faster, faster, faster. At the speed of light, we can do what folks 100 years ago did at about 25 knots, if they were lucky and had good wind in their sails.

No matter how fast we move, no matter how fast we get things done, it's never enough. We want to go faster and faster, yet one thing never changes. Most of us are still harried, hurried, stressed out and close to burnout.

You'd think that with all this speed, we'd have more time to rest, take it easy and chill out. It makes sense that if you get something done quicker, you should have more time for yourself.

So how many of us have more time to rest, relax, do our own thing, and spend with family and friends doing what we like? How many people do you hear complaining about having too much time on their hands? Have you ever heard someone say, "With my super fast computer working so fast, I have so much spare time I don't know what to do with myself"? or "Because I can do my business by email, I have so much free time now"? Have you ever heard someone claim "Because I can travel from city to city in just a few hours, instead of days or weeks, I have plenty of time to rest and relax"?

It doesn't happen because in this day and age of instant everything, we feel more pressed for time than ever before.

It could be turned into a mathematical formula: if we call the speed at which we move and get things done "s" and the time we have after "s" we call "q," our formula reads thus: the greater "s," the less "q." Translated, this means that the faster we move and the quicker we can get things done, the less time we have.

The sad thing is that the faster we move, the more we need to rest.

We're moving and doing things at speeds our ancestor would have deemed miraculous —even supernatural. But with all this speed and technology, if the day had 30 hours instead of 24 we'd still complain that we need more time.

THE REST COMMANDMENT

All this leads to where we were in the previous chapter—the Ten Commandments. We now understand how much pain and suffering comes from violating these commandments, and how relevant they are for us today. Far from being antiquated, if people would obey these commandments it would make the world a better place.

One of these 10 commandments is all about rest. God, our Creator, commands us to take time off from our lives to slow down, relax and take it easy. If that was important thousands of years ago, when the pace of life was somewhat less intense than it is now, how much more important is it to us today?

Back then, the fastest a human could go was probably no faster than the fastest chariot. While we move so fast today, we still don't have time to get the rest we need.

This is precisely why God gave humanity the Sabbath—a day of rest.

Doesn't the word "rest" sound so nice? Imagine having the time to rest, slow down and take stock of things. Imagine the chance to do something other than try and make money to get ahead in life. Imagine the chance to be free from the hustle and bustle, just for a little while, to have time to be with family and friends.

Rest is what the Sabbath commandment is all about. It's so relevant, needed and timely for us today.

THE GORDON GEKKO FACTOR

For starters, let's take a look at the Sabbath commandment itself. It's the fourth commandment and some say it's like a hinge connecting the first three commandments—about our relationship with God—with the last six—about our relationship with others.

As we'll soon discover, Sabbath is about both.

"Remember the Sabbath day, to keep it holy. Six days you shall labour and do all your work, but the seventh day is the Sabbath of the Lord your God. In it you shall do no work: you, nor your son, nor your daughter, nor your male servant, nor your female servant, nor your cattle, nor your stranger who is within your gates. For in six days the Lord made the heavens and the earth, the sea, and all that is in them, and rested the seventh day. Therefore the Lord blessed the Sabbath day and hallowed it" (Exodus 20:8–11).

There's a lot of information in this text so let's focus on the practical aspect of it first.

The first thing it says is to do "no work." That doesn't mean a little bit or half a day's work. It doesn't mean a few phone calls to the office or a quick teleconference before chilling out. It means no work at all for the day, whatsoever. In the previous chapter, we saw that the commandments were a kind of protection. They protected us from things like murder, adultery and stealing, and all the heartache and suffering that follows them.

In a similar way, the Sabbath is also a protection. It protects us, more often than not, from ourselves—from our own greed and ambition. It saves us from our lust for more and more, and our unending desire to take from the world around us.

Have you ever observed the people who work all the time in order to make more and more money? They work around the clock to get more and more things, then burnout so they can't enjoy them. How many people allow themselves to become trapped in their own world of greed?

In 1886, Russian author Leo Tolstoy wrote a short story called "How Much Land Does a Man Need?" In it, a struggling farmer named Pahom thinks, "If I had plenty of land, I shouldn't fear the Devil himself."

The Devil himself, listening in, silently replies: "We will have a tussle. I'll give you land enough; and by means of that land I will get you into my power."

After acquiring land, selling land and constantly restarting in new places with more land, Pahom hears about Bashkirs—people who sell land cheaply. Pahom goes there and they offer him land for "a thousand rubles a day." He is told that as far as he can walk in one day, that's the amount of land he can buy for his 1000 rubles. The land would be his on one condition: "If you don't return," they said, "on the same day to the spot whence you started, your money is lost."

Thrilled, Pahom takes off walking, stopping now and then to mark off the edges of the rich, virgin soil that would soon be his. He keeps going and going, as far as he possibly can before making a turn. Though he had covered a lot of land, he soon realises he must get back or he'll have no land at all.

Drained and exhausted, Pahom sees he is running out of time. The sun is almost setting and if he isn't back soon, all will be lost. In a panic, he starts to run as fast as he can. He runs and runs and, just as he reaches the point where he started, Pahom collapses—dead.

"The Bashkirs clicked their tongues to show their pity."

Tolstoy ended his story like this:

"His servant picked up the spade and dug a grave long enough for Pahom to lie in, and buried him in it. Six feet from his head to his heels was all he needed."

You may remember the movie *Wall Street* (1987) with Michael Douglas as the take-no-prisoners rich guy, Gordon Gekko. He's the character who just wants more and more, with the famous line, "Greed is good."

Gekko's character was based on a real person—a Wall Street tycoon named Ivan Boesky. In 1986, he was the centre of a major Wall Street financial scandal because his greed eventually got him locked up. Prior to this event, he gave a speech at the University of California at Berkeley. Boesky famously said, "I think greed is healthy. You can be greedy and still feel good about yourself."

Perhaps getting arrested changed his mind about just how "healthy" greed is. In the movie, Gekko also had another memorable line:

"Lunch," he said, "is for wimps."

This is because making money and buying things takes time. Who wants to waste that time eating?

In contrast stands the Sabbath—a weekly break in the vicious weekly cycle that could swallow us up in our own avarice.

The Sabbath tells us that enough is enough. Life is more than just work and more than just making money.

The very presence of the Sabbath tells us not to let greed, avarice and the desire for wealth dominate us. Sure, we need to work to live but we also need to rest.

The Sabbath is a weekly reminder that there's more to our existence than just getting ahead, making a buck and climbing the ladder.

Rest—it's what the Sabbath is all about.

Here's how one writer expressed his experience with the Sabbath and family:

> I love to walk with my boy through the wooded trails where we live. We can take our time and enjoy what we see because there's no rush to meet business appointments or to turn on my word processor. Nothing secular is allowed to intrude. My two-year-old son loves to run and yell and laugh and collect sticks and rocks and fallen apples. The richest, happiest, most precious moments of my existence have been on Sabbath afternoons, where I have the freedom to frolic leisurely with my son. Few sounds touch my heart more than his uninhibited shrieks and laughter as he romps free like a little lamb. Sabbath gives us a sacred break, valued beyond money.

Some things are more valuable than money. The Sabbath helps us understand what these things are and offers us the protection to enjoy them as we should.

WEEKLY SABBATICAL

Now that we've looked at the first part of the commandment, let's read it again:

"Remember the Sabbath day, to keep it holy. Six days you shall labour and do all your work, but the seventh day is the Sabbath of the Lord your God. In it you shall do no work: you, nor your son, nor your daughter, nor your male servant, nor your female servant, nor your cattle, nor your stranger who is within your gates. For in six days the Lord made the heavens and the earth, the sea, and all that is in them, and rested the seventh day. Therefore the Lord blessed the Sabbath day and hallowed it" (Exodus 20:8–11).

While most of us don't have male or female servants, cattle or strangers in our gates, the principle still stands. It's showing just how pervasive this rest can be if you create an atmosphere of rest in your home. Don't let someone come in and ruin the sense of rest during your special, holy time. Or, to use a common phrase, this is your "quality time" to spend with God, family and others you care about in a relaxing, restful atmosphere.

It is said that the average American father spends about 37 seconds a day in one-on-one interaction with each of his children. Who cares how much quality is in 37 seconds? This isn't anywhere near enough time to be meaningful.

One thing is for sure, though: for families who keep the Sabbath, the amount of time together as a family works out as a lot more than 37 seconds. Sometimes, people in the office might tell someone, "Look, I'm spending the day with my wife, or children, so don't call me for anything short of an emergency."

With the Sabbath, God is doing the same thing for us. He has set this quality time aside for you to build your family relationships or any other relationships. Or maybe, He knows you just need to rest and mentally, physically, and spiritually reset in a weekly sabbatical. God has good reason for commanding us to do this.

Notice that the word "sabbatical" comes directly from "Sabbath."

Again, look at the frantic pace of our lives and how hard we work. We're running on all cylinders, afraid to slow down because someone might get ahead of us in this race to nowhere. After all, we run and run to cross the finish line first and what happens after that? What have we accomplished? How long does the satisfaction last anyway?

The Sabbath is a way of rebelling against all of that—a way of showing we can be free from the trap of running a pointless race. Some things are just more important. God put the command to rest right up there with the command against stealing, murder and adultery. That's pretty heavy, if you think about it. Clearly, God deems this weekly rest to be important.

That's likely because life is full of stress. Who doesn't feel close to burnout at times? Again, the faster we are moving, the easier it is to burnout, wear down and run yourself into the ground.

According to an article in the *New York Times:*

> "Prolonged or severe stress has been shown to weaken the immune system, strain the heart, damage memory cells in the brain and deposit fat at the waist rather than the hips and buttocks (a risk factor for heart disease, cancer and other illnesses)," said Dr Bruce S McEwen, director of the neuroendocrinology laboratory at Rockefeller University and the author of a new book, *The End of Stress as We Know It.* "Stress has been implicated in aging, depression, heart disease, rheumatoid arthritis and diabetes, among other illnesses."

The Sabbath offers us a weekly respite from all our cares. Without exception, the Sabbath comes every week with an invitation from God. As the sun sets every Friday night, it's God's way of saying," It's time to rest and relax now. Take this time to trust in Me and put away the things of the world. Take it easy in Me and use our time together to rebuild physically, mentally and spiritually."

History has seen various failed attempts to re-format the seven-day week. During the French Revolution, the authorities tried to abolish the day of rest by introducing a 10-day work week. It failed when the people rebelled and reverted to the traditional ordering of the week. During World War II in England, the heads of a factory wanted more production so they created a 10-day work week. The irony is that before long, less was produced than before. The workers needed a weekly rest.

When God tells us to take time out, He knows what He is talking about. After all, He is our Creator.

MORE THAN DNA

This leads to another important aspect of the Sabbath. The commandment itself gives us a reason for taking the Sabbath rest: "For in six days the Lord made the heavens and the earth, the sea, and all that is in them, and rested the seventh day. Therefore the Lord blessed the Sabbath day and hallowed it" (Exodus 20:11).

Amid all the experiential and relational benefits of keeping the Sabbath, it's also there to remind us that we are beings created by God. Every week, we are reminded that our existence isn't by chance. We are here and our lives are here for a purpose.

English writer Mary Anne Evans, better known by her pen name George Eliot, wrote:

> Against atheism, which denies the existence of a personal God; against materialism, which denies that this visible universe has it roots in the unseen; and against secularism, which denies the need to worship, the Sabbath is an eternal witness. It symbolically commemorates the creative power which spoke all things into being, the wisdom which ordered the adaptations and harmony, the love which made, as well as pronounced, all "very good." It is set as a perpetual guardian of man against that spiritual infirmity which has everywhere led him to a denial of the Creator who made him, or to the degradation of that God into a creature made with his own hands.

We all need our weekly reminder as we are bombarded over and over in the media with the idea that we are nothing but chance beings. The press seems to take it for granted that we are the result of mindless and purposeless forces that accidentally created us. Isn't that the gist of the whole evolutionary model of human origins?

Years ago, arch-atheist Richard Dawkins wrote a book called *The Selfish Gene*. In it, he argues that humans are nothing but "survival machines"—beings whose sole purpose is to ensure the survival of their genes. According to Dawkins, Darwin got it wrong. He argued that evolution wasn't to keep the species around but to keep the genes around, flowing from generation to generation. As a chicken is just an egg's way of making more eggs, humans are just the gene's way of making more genes. From a biological perspective, humans are the means, not the ends. It seems that the ends are more genes and more DNA—that's all.

In the words of British comedy troupe Monty Python, we are all "simply spiralling coils of self-replicating DNA."

Can this really be the answer? Can DNA and genes explain all our desires, hopes, joys, pain and disappointments? Does the idea of being "simply spiralling coils of DNA" bring meaning, purpose and fulfilment to our lives? Is this the key to unlocking the hard questions about why we are here? If this is the answer to the deepest mysteries, does that make everything alright because we now know?

This view is not very satisfactory. Even if we can't prove it, it just doesn't seem adequate. It would be like someone trying to explain the beauty of dance through muscle anatomy and physiology—and nothing more.

Then the Sabbath comes, a weekly reminder—one seventh of our lives—to tell us we are more than just "spiralling coils of DNA." In a special way, we are beings created in the image of God. We were made for a reason and there is a God who loves us, cares about us and wants us to rest in Him.

Even if they don't know anything else about the Bible, most people know the opening line: "In the beginning God created the heavens and the earth" (Genesis 1:1). Note that the line says nothing about some of the things we have already considered. It says nothing about the great controversy between Christ and Satan, and nothing about Jesus dying on the cross. It says nothing about the law of God and nothing about the Second Coming.

That's because all the teachings we have talked about so far mean nothing apart from the fact that God created us. This point is so crucial that God has given us a weekly reminder, called the Sabbath. More than anything else, it points to our creation. It is because on this great truth all the others truths exist.

THE INVINCIBLE DAY

God has commanded that we spend one-seventh of our lives remembering that He is our Creator. This is something He didn't do for any other Christian teaching simply because no other Christian teaching has validity apart from this one. That's how important this idea is.

In every world religion, people revere something—shrines, cities and even other people. They kiss holy land and they immerse themselves in holy water. Their ears clutch the syllables of holy men.

However, the first thing the Bible's Book of Genesis declares holy is not a hill, shrine or place. It's a block of time—the seventh day: "Then God blessed the seventh day and sanctified it, because in it He rested from all His work which God had created and made" (Genesis 2:3).

The word "sanctified" comes from a word that means "to set apart for holy use." Though Creation dealt with the heavens, the earth, the birds, the sea and the beasts of the earth, which are all things of space, God pronounced time—not space—blessed and holy. This makes sense because besides space, time is the dimension in which God's creation—the heavens, the earth, the birds, the sea and the beasts of the earth—exist.

If God had made one specific place holy—a hill, a spring or a city—then only certain people would have easy access to it. Everyone would have to travel to that one special place in order to worship. Thankfully time comes to us, rather than us going to it. Once a week, as the earth rotates on its axis, the Sabbath circles the globe. Arriving on one sundown and leaving on the next, the seventh day washes over the planet like a huge cleansing wave.

We never have to seek it because the day always finds us!

Meanwhile, look at history. We know that though holy cities can be burned, holy people can be killed and holy shrines can be looted, time is beyond all that. No-one can touch time—you can smash all the clocks in the world but time still marches on, out of our reach even though we are immersed in it.

By making a special time holy, God has made the Sabbath invincible. He's placed it in an element that transcends any devices of humanity. Armies can ransack cities and rulers can ban pilgrimages but no-one can keep the seventh day away.

We can no more stop the Sabbath than we can stop the sunrise. God protected His memorial to the objects of space by placing it in time, which is not vulnerable to man.

Finally, humans can avoid holy things—they can hide from objects, people and places but they can't flee from time. We can ignore it, be ignorant of it or hate it but the Sabbath always comes—and nothing and no-one can stop it.

Holding out hope for all, the Sabbath stands as the universal yet invincible memorial of God's work in making humankind. Framed in time—the most basic element of God's creation—the Sabbath points us to the essence of our existence. More than any other biblical symbol, it communicates that we are the handiwork of God. As the prime symbol of our roots, the Sabbath tells us who we are, why we are and where we are going—all in the space of 24 hours.

Only those who choose to keep the Sabbath can know for themselves what a blessing it is.

THE NECKLACE

Years ago, Frenchman Guy de Maupassant wrote a short story called "The Necklace." It was about a young French woman who married a typical, normal guy—a clerk.

The woman, Madame Matilda Loisel, felt bitter about this existence. She dreamed of "quiet antechambers, with their Oriental hangings, lighted by high, bronze torches" and "of large drawing rooms, hung in old silks." Matilda was daily reminded that she had "neither frocks nor jewels, nothing. And she loved only these things."

Then one day the clerk came home with a card—an invitation to an elegant ball at which "Mr and Mrs Loisel's company" was requested. At first, she refused the invitation. But after great expense in getting her a new dress and borrowing a fancy necklace from a friend, the clerk and his wife attended the ball.

"Mme Loisel was a great success. She was the prettiest of all, elegant, gracious, smiling and full of joy. All the men noticed her, asked her name and wanted to be presented. All the members of the Cabinet wished to waltz with her. The Minister of Education paid her some attention."

She luxuriated in "the triumph of her beauty, in the glory of her success," dancing until four in the morning, while the clerk fell asleep in another room at about midnight. Not long after leaving, they discovered that she had lost the borrowed necklace. After searching frantically for days, they knew they would never find the necklace.

What could they tell the owner of the necklace? After stalling the return for as long as possible, the clerk finally found an exact copy of the necklace—for 36,000 francs. Such an amount would surely destroy them financially.

> He borrowed it, asking for a thousand francs of one, five hundred of another, five louis of this one, and three louis of that one. He gave notes, made ruinous promises, and took money of usurers and the whole race of lenders. He compromised his whole existence, in fact, risked his signature, without even knowing whether he could make it good or not, and, harassed by anxiety for the future, by the black misery which surrounded him, and the prospect of all physical privation and moral torture, he went to get the necklace, depositing on the merchants counter thirty-six thousand francs.

For a decade every centime, every sou paid against the debt drained something out of them until all that remained was a bleached dry woman and a man so thin he barely held a shadow. "At the end of ten years, they had restored all, all, with interest of the usurer, and accumulated interest besides."

Then one Sunday, on the Champs-Elysées, Matilda saw Mrs Forestier—the one from whom she borrowed the necklace—"still young, still pretty, still attractive," walking with a child. Mrs Forestier didn't recognise the haggard woman who stopped her on the street. It was only after Matilda explained who she was that Mrs Forestier asked what had happened to her.

Matilda said she looked so bad because she and the clerk had ruined their lives in order to replace the lost necklace. After hearing the whole wretched story, Mrs Forestier looked at Matilda and said, incredulously:

> "You say that you bought a diamond necklace to replace mine?"

> "Yes. You did not perceive it then? They were just alike."

> And she smiled with a proud and simple joy. Madame Forestier was touched and took both her hands as she replied: "Oh! My poor Matilda! Mine were false. They were not worth over five hundred francs!"

We all have our own stories to tell and most of us work pretty hard—even to the point of burnout. What are we working so hard for? Do we want our stories to end like the Loisels'?

No, we do not want them to end so pointlessly. We can choose to live for more important things that actually matter—as God wants us to. Because He doesn't want us to burnout in the process, He gave us the gift of the Sabbath.

First, it helps us know what our lives are really about by pointing us to God as our Creator. All other truths flow from this one great truth, including what's important in life, what really matters and what's worth striving for.

Second, it helps us not burn out during our striving. Amid the hustle and bustle of life, the Sabbath gives us rest.

As Jesus Himself said, "Come to me, all you who labour and are heavy laden, and I will give you rest" (Matthew 11:28).

The gift of the Sabbath is one practical way we can receive this rest.

forgery

In 2008, three Long Island, USA, high-school students were arrested for printing counterfeit $10s, $20s and $50s. The 17-year-old culprits used ink jet printers in "the back of a pickup truck" to print the bills.

Amazingly, police say the power source was a Radio Shack inverter plugged into the vehicle's cigarette lighter.

You would think any teenager using the tray of a small truck as a factory floor and inkjet printers to output bogus bills would get caught and arrested in no time.

However, reports indicate the teens may have been circulating counterfeit money for an incredible two years.

The idea of the teens getting away with it for two years is extraordinary in itself. But if three 17 year olds could do it, imagine the potential if a malevolent nation or a sophisticated group of international criminals figured it out.

One thing we can be certain of is the kids in the back of the truck weren't printing $3 or even $30 bills. No other counterfeiters would either. This is because the first rule of something fake or counterfeit is to make it appear as similar to the genuine as possible. Wouldn't it get a little suspicious if someone handed them a $3 note?

The Reserve Bank of Australia says, "While Australia's counterfeiting rate is very low, the following guide is provided to help you identify a genuine Australian banknote. To determine if a suspect banknote is a counterfeit, it is best to compare it with a banknote that is known to be genuine."

It's an important principle: the best way to determine if something is not genuine is to compare it with what is known to be real.

Of course, counterfeit cash is only one kind of forgery. There are plenty of other things that claim to be real.

CATCH ME IF YOU CAN

Most people have never heard of Frank Abagnale, Jr, which is exactly how Mr Abagnale liked it. From the time he was a teenager until his early 30s, he was one of the most successful con men, forgers and impostors in the world. His story was so amazing it was eventually made into a movie directed by Steven Spielberg. *Catch Me If You Can* (2002) starred Tom Hanks as the cop who chased and caught him, and Leonard DiCaprio as the notorious Abagnale himself.

During one of his many cons, Abagnale posed as a doctor in a Georgia hospital—not just a doctor but the supervisor of a whole wing of doctors. He pulled off this impersonation for more than two years. The role of supervisor was actually perfect because, in this position, he rarely had to do any medical work. All he had to do was supervise other doctors, who did the actual medical procedures. He spent most of his time looking at charts and scribbling his signature on them. No-one suspected a thing until an infant almost died from oxygen deprivation. This was because Abagnale—or, as he was known there, "Frank Connors, MD"—had no idea what a "blue baby" was.

For years, a supposed faith healer and evangelist named Peter Popoff would go around the United States and do "miracles." Standing before the audience, he would recite the names of people in the crowd. He might also name some of their sicknesses, give their address or tell them the names of their relatives. He claimed the Lord has revealed these things to him and that these people were being called out for "special healing."

Imagine if you had some terrible sickness like cancer. You go to a meeting and someone you've never met stands on the stage, calls you by name, and is even able to tell you your address and disease. No-one would blame you if you thought, Hmmm, maybe God really is talking to me through this person! Maybe God really will heal me miraculously.

It turns out that Popoff's miracles needed a little technological help. Someone got suspicious when they noticed the reverend was wearing a hearing aid. They thought, Why would a man who can cure all sorts of serious ailments, like cancer, need a hearing aid for himself?

It was discovered that his wife, Elizabeth, was helping him. She would sit in the audience, talking to people and getting the information. She would then repeat it via a hidden radio back to her husband standing on the stage. The "Lord" was communicating to Peter Popoff through a 39.17 MHz secret transmitter and receiver. Elizabeth had the transmitter hidden in her blouse and Popoff had the receiver in his ear—the "hearing aid." Acting as if the personal information were coming to him directly from the throne of God, Popoff would get these poor people up on the stage and supposedly heal them right then and there.

Perhaps the most horrifically consequential example of religious fraud deals with the young jihads. Potential suicides are given great encouragement and moral support from elders who will not become martyrs themselves. They tell these young candidates that on the Day of Judgment, women bombers will be allowed to pick 72 relatives to also enter paradise with them. The males, of course, are promised their 72 celestial virgins. These young people are told, "You die to achieve Allah's satisfaction. You have been chosen by Allah because he has seen all that is good in you."

Thus, these unfortunate young people are brainwashed and programmed to kill themselves and as many others as possible. So many sad deaths are based on the fakery, fraud and deception of a radical wing of Islam who, regardless of how sincere (maybe) they may be, keep sending them to their deaths.

FAKES, FAKES AND MORE FAKES

We live in a world where fakery and fraud are all around us. Everywhere we look, we see fake photoshopped pictures and fake IDs. It's easy to get fake diplomas and fake artwork. Fake websites try and fool people into giving up their passwords and usernames. Fake religious healers and fake herbal remedies claim to relieve pain and promise amazing results. People sell fake watches, fake jewellery, fake handbags and fake brand-name shoes. There's also fake prescription drugs, fake biographies, fake paintings and fake DVDs.

If there's money to be made, someone's going to try and fake it.

So far, we've looked at the great controversy between good and evil—between Christ and Satan. We've seen how this conflict plays out in the world and in our own lives. Our stories are often expressed and lived out in the midst of this battle. There are always choices to be made as we question what is right and what is wrong. Even if we think we know what is right, we often struggle with how to do it.

Just like in our experiences in the world, we have to deal with fakes in this battle, too. But this time, believing the fakes has eternal consequences. In 2 Corinthians 11:12–14, the apostle Paul writes, "But what I do, I will also continue to do, that I may cut off the opportunity from those who desire an opportunity to be regarded just as we are in the things of which they boast. For such are false apostles, deceitful workers, transforming themselves into apostles of Christ. And no wonder! For Satan himself transforms himself into an angel of light."

Without going into the context of this verse, let's note that while Paul is discussing fakes and frauds, he's talking about both human frauds—those who claim to be apostles of Christ but aren't—as well as supernatural frauds. He's talking about Satan, a literal being, who masquerades as "an angel of light."

Satan seeks to deceive us by pretending to be what he is not. The Bible has a lot to say about Satan's deceptiveness:

- "And war broke out in heaven: Michael and his angels fought with the dragon; and the dragon and his angels fought, but they did not prevail, nor was a place found for them in heaven any longer. So the great dragon was cast out, that serpent of old, called the Devil and Satan, who deceives the whole world; he was cast to the earth, and his angels were cast out with him" (Revelation 12:7–9).

- "You are of your father the devil, and the desires of your father you want to do. He was a murderer from the beginning, and does not stand in the truth, because there is no truth in him. When he speaks a lie, he speaks from his own resources, for he is a liar and the father of it" (John 8:44).

He's had a lot of time to perfect deceiving the whole world. Even the most faithful follower of Jesus is deceived by the devil to some degree. Part of his deception is to use fraud and fakery, replacing the real with a counterfeit.

The biblical depiction of Satan, taken from the Old Testament, describes Satan this way:

> How you are fallen from heaven, O Lucifer, son of the morning! How you are cut down to the ground, you who weakened the nations! For you have said in your heart: "I will ascend into heaven, I will exalt my throne above the stars of God; I will also sit on the mount of the congregation on the farthest sides of the north; I will ascend above the heights of the clouds, I will be like the Most High" (Isaiah 14:12–14).

Take note of the last part, where Satan wants to "be like the Most High." He wants to pretend to be what he is not—he's a fake and a forger for even trying to be God.

Part of his lie in deceiving the whole world is through the way he creates fakes and counterfeits. He does this to keep us from knowing God because Satan does not want us to know Jesus. He doesn't want us to know the Lord personally and have a relationship with Him. He does not want us to have the promise of eternal life that God offers us. This is the heart of the great controversy.

FAKE CHRISTS

> Then if anyone says to you, "Look, here is the Christ!" or "There!" do not believe it. For false christs and false prophets will rise and show great signs and wonders to deceive, if possible, even the elect. See, I have told you beforehand. Therefore

if they say to you, "Look, He is in the desert!" do not go out; or "Look, He is in the inner rooms!" do not believe it (Matthew 24:23–26).

Jesus warned us about those who would come and impersonate Him—every one of them nothing more than false christs, false prophets, shams and conmen.

It's a pretty bold prediction for a man who lived almost 2000 years ago and never had a large following while alive. From a human standpoint, He never amounted to much at all—He never commanded an army or led a nation. Jesus was crucified at a young age by the Romans—just one of an untold number of Jews murdered in the same way.

A lot religious people lived back then, all claiming to be the Messiah. If they were so special, why haven't we heard about them today? Other than Jesus, no other names have lasted. Not only do we know His name but just as He said, people have come claiming to be Him. It would be like a street preacher today saying that, after he died, all through the following centuries folks would arise insisting that they were him. Why should anyone take him seriously?

But this is exactly what has happened with the itinerant preacher, Jesus of Nazareth. People have come, and still do—all fakes—claiming to be Jesus, just as He predicted.

One of the more colourful fakes lives in the Miami area. His name is José Luis de Jesús Miranda, who was born in 1946 in Ponce, Puerto Rico. A former heroin addict, convicted criminal and divorced father of four, Miranda claims to be Jesus Christ. He has followers all through Latin America and parts of the United States, who are convinced He really is Jesus.

Luis de Jesus Miranda, aka Jesus, even made an appearance on the *Today Show* in New York City, where he was clear about his true identity. He told the *Today Show* host, right to her face, "I am Jesus Christ man, in front of you."

He also got about six minutes on the Glenn Beck show as well. While interviewing him, Beck said, "It is weird that Jesus said he would come as a thief in the night, and that you have been arrested for petty theft."

Miranda's ministry has been very lucrative, too. At one point, this Jesus Christ lived in an expensive house, owned a $142,000 watch, and drove both a 7-series BMW and an armoured Lexus.

The scariest thing isn't someone claiming to be Jesus but that people actually believe him!

THE FAKE COMMANDMENT

In this context of religious fakes and forgery, the apostle Paul wrote:

> Let no-one deceive you by any means; for that Day will not come unless the falling away comes first, and the man of sin is revealed, the son of perdition, who opposes and exalts himself above all that is called God or that is worshiped, so that he sits as God in the temple of God, showing himself that he is God (2 Thessalonians 2:3, 4).

This "someone" is a fraud, claiming to be what he isn't—claiming to be God.

The Reserve Bank of Australia's recommendation of comparison with the genuine, meaning what is real, means there can be no counterfeits without something real to be copied. The only reason a fake $20 bill can fool someone is because there are genuine ones out there. The only way someone can be fooled by a fake Jesus is because many believe a true One exists. If no-one believed in Jesus, no-one would fake being Him.

This leads into what is one of the greatest and most prevalent religious fakes in all of human history. It's one that billions follow—unwittingly, in most cases—and have been doing so for centuries. This might seem unimportant on the surface but it has powerful implications.

We now know about the Ten Commandments and how people often think they are an outdated, antiquated moral code from an ancient civilisation that has nothing to do with us today. We now know just how tragically wrong-headed this reaction is. Violating just one of the Ten Commandments often leads to terrible pain and suffering—for those who choose to disobey, and for their friends and family. We acknowledged that one of the most neglected yet important commandments is the Sabbath—a weekly chance to rest, recuperate, recharge and remember that we are here because God had created us. More than any other commandment, the Sabbath also points us back to God as our Creator. It is a weekly reminder to us that we are here—not through evolution and not because space aliens came down and seeded the world—but because a loving God created us in His image.

This brings us right back to the beginning of everything—to the Creation story itself, the foundation of the world and where life on earth began:

> Then God saw everything that He had made, and indeed it was very good. So the evening and the morning were the sixth day. Thus the heavens and the earth, and all the host of them, were finished. And on the seventh day God ended His work which He had done, and He rested on the seventh day from all His work which He had

done. Then God blessed the seventh day and sanctified it, because in it He rested from all His work which God had created and made (Genesis 1:31–2:3).

As far as humans are concerned, this takes us as far back as we can go. To get behind the Creation is to get to the Creator, God Himself!

The most basic, fundamental symbol of Creation, the foundation for everything else in all of these texts, is the seventh-day Sabbath.

Notice that it's the seventh day—not the first day or the third day, nor any other day but the seventh.

In many languages, the word for "Saturday" actually comes directly from the word "Sabbath."

Which day of the week is the biblical Sabbath? Many are confused over the issue, but such confusion is unnecessary. Not only is the answer plain from history and the Bible, it is also clear from the names for the seventh day of the week, Saturday, in many languages.

For example, the Spanish word for the seventh day of the week, Saturday, is sabado—the same word for "Sabbath." In fact, in more than 100 ancient and modern languages the seventh day of the week was named "Sabbath" or its equivalent. Following is a list of names for the seventh day of the week, Saturday, in 24 languages in which the root word Sabbath is still easily recognisable. . . .

Arabic: Sabet
Armenian: Shabat
Bosnian: Subota
Bulgarian: Sabota
Corsican: Sàbatu
Croatian: Subota
Czech: Sobota
Georgian: Sabati
Greek: Savvato
Indonesian: Sabtu
Italian: Sabato
Latin: Sabbatum
Maltese: is-Sibt
Polish: Sobota
Portuguese: Sábado
Romanian: Sambata

Russian: Subbota
Serbian: Subota
Slovak: Sobota
Slovene: Sobota
Somali: Sabti
Spanish: Sabado
Sudanese: Saptu
Ukrainian: Subota*

THE FAKE SABBATH

Despite these 24 examples of languages reflecting which day is the Sabbath, there's a slight problem. The vast majority of Christians worship on Sunday, the first day of the week. Everywhere you look, church sign after church sign calls people to worship services on Sunday. Why don't they call them to worship on Saturday, the seventh day—the one day that the Creation account itself documents, pointing to God as the Creator? Your first reaction may be "Big deal! What does it matter?"

But if you think about it for a moment, you may remember that the seventh-day is the biblical symbol—the foundational sign of God as Creator and as God Himself. Embedded at the very beginning of the story of Creation is this sign, the seventh-day. You can't go any further back without going to God Himself.

To usurp this sign of God as Creator is to usurp the role of God Himself.

From what we've noted so far about Satan, he has been trying to usurp the role of God for a long, long time. What better way is there to usurp the role of God than to try and usurp the sign of His creative power?

This is exactly what has happened with the change of the seventh-day Sabbath—the day specifically written in the Bible as the sign of God's creatorship—to Sunday, a day God has never commanded anyone to keep.

We're not saying that the millions of folks who go to church on Sunday are consciously seeking to usurp the role of God as Creator. Of course they're not—most simply don't know. But ignorance of a truth doesn't make the error truth. The belief that there's no global warming,

*From < www.beyondtoday.tv/booklets/SS/names-sabbath-language.asp>.

no matter how sincere, doesn't mean there's no global warming. The belief of Holocaust deniers that the Holocaust never happened doesn't mean the Nazis didn't murder millions. In the same way, the fact that the vast majority of Christians are violating one of God's specific commandments doesn't mean the fourth commandment is invalid.

We need to acknowledge that there are deep issues here. The sign of God's creative power is the seventh-day, and we now understand that to usurp that sign is really to usurp the role and authority of God as God. Although most people don't think of it this way, we can be sure that the one who has been trying to usurp that authority all along in the great controversy—the devil—certainly does.

THE SEAL

During the 2008 presidential election in the United States, the Obama campaign caused a bit of a ruckus when someone in his party created their own version of a presidential seal for candidate Barak Obama—the sign or symbol of the presidency.

Some people really went after him for daring to display something so presumptuous. Even though it was obviously not the presidential seal, it came close enough in symbolising the power, authority and office of the President of the United States. At that time, Obama didn't have the right to claim that power, authority or office. It was seen as a usurpation of a position he didn't hold. Even though it was just an inexact symbol, it still caused a negative reaction.

Just imagine if the Obama campaign had made one that looked just like the real one! That would have really caused a stir—and rightly so.

It's easy to parallel this idea with the "replacement" of the seventh-day Sabbath. Just as the Obama party's fake presidential seal did not make Obama president, God's original sign of His creative power and authority can't be replaced with the first day, as this is symbolic of another power seeking to usurp the place of God Himself. Thinking about this, we can begin to understand why the issues go deeper than which day someone goes to church.

As part of this great controversy, we have all been victims of fraud in one way or another. Ironically enough, the Reserve Bank of Australia gave us the answer to protect us from so much of the fraud out there. Simply put, we need to know and recognise the genuine.

This is good advice, both for money and also in the spiritual realm.

the dead zone

For the residents of Marina del Ray in California, it was just another macabre Halloween display. The Halloween season for 2009 had all the usual stuff—fake bodies made of straw hanging from trees on front lawns, carved pumpkin lanterns in windows and plastic skeletons decorating front porches. It's the type of foolishness that would make you think the people who put it there were warped if it happened at any other time of year.

Being the Halloween season, no-one thought much of the body sitting on the balcony outside an apartment. A lot of people saw it—neighbours in other apartments and people on the street—but never gave it a second thought. Mostly they appreciated that it looked like someone had shot him in the head—a nicely gruesome effect.

The only problem was that after the Halloween revelry ended, this body remained. People noticed that something was starting to smell. Though the apartment building itself overlooked a marina, this wasn't the stink of a dead tuna floating among the docks.

Getting suspicious, someone finally alerted the authorities. Much to everyone's surprise and horror, the body was the corpse of the man who had lived there—an apparent suicide victim named Mr Mostafa Mahmoud Zayed, 75. The gaping hole in his eye wasn't part of the Halloween festivities—it was where he shot himself in the head.

Halloween is a strange tradition because for 364 days of the year, we mourn and fear death. But for some reason, millions of people reach back to an ancient Celt festival known as Samhain (pronounced sow-in) and all but celebrate death on that night, whether they realise it or not.

How many of us would voluntarily celebrate death if that is what we knew we were doing?

FOR WHOM THE BELL TOLLS

However much we try to mask it, we all live with the awareness that death could happen at any moment. It could take any one of us, just like that.

All our hopes, dreams, plans and desires vanish. We disintegrate into bones and chemicals that, over time, break down into nothing. There's something wrong when our gravestones outlast our bones.

Of course, most of us know people who have been sick and, as expected, die. That's bad enough but who among us hasn't been with someone, doing what they do every day, only to hear the next day that that person is dead?

The shock, disbelief, suddenness and finality of it all shakes us to the core. It should because we know that tomorrow it could be you, or me, or one of our loved ones.

John Donne's famous poem from his *Meditations*, "For Whom the Bell Tolls," sums it up nicely:

"No man is an island, entire of itself. Each is a piece of the continent, a part of the main. If a clod be washed away by the sea, Europe is the less. As well as if a promontory were. As well as if a manor of thine own or of thine friend's were. Each man's death diminishes me, for I am involved in mankind. Therefore, send not to know for whom the bell tolls, it tolls for thee."

The bells will toll for each of us sooner or later and there's nothing we can do to stop it.

Modern medicine has done wonders so we might be able to put it off a little more. Life expectancy has risen over the centuries, at least in some places. But even so, it's only by 10, 20 or 30 years. This is a huge step forward and who wouldn't want those extra years if they could get them? But in the great scheme of things, what's 10, 20 or 30 years when eternity stretches out before them?

Part of our story is all about dealing with death. We need to learn to cope with not just the prospect of our own—which we will all have to deal with in one way or another—but with the death we see all around us. The death that touches us scares us—it is hard to understand and comes in so many strange ways.

Most people don't know the name of Tsutomu Yamaguchi, who died of stomach cancer on January 4, 2010. He was 93, which is amazing enough. But what was truly amazing about him is that he survived both atomic bomb blasts over Japan.

It was 8:15 am when Mr Yamaguchi was on his way to work on the morning of August 6, 1945. He was making his way toward the shipyard when the "Little Boy" nuclear bomb detonated over Hiroshima. He was a few miles from ground zero but it still ruptured his eardrums and burned his upper torso.

After spending the night in a bomb shelter, Mr Yamaguchi returned to his hometown of Nagasaki. He was in his office telling his boss about the Hiroshima blast when "suddenly the same white light filled the room." He was not injured by this second blast.

"I thought," he told interviewers later, "that the mushroom cloud had followed me from Hiroshima." He survived twice, while untold thousands died.

Death is hard to understand and more than a little frightening, too.

In "The Love Song of J Alfred Prufrock," poet T S Eliot wrote:

And I have seen the eternal Footman hold my coat, and snicker,
And in short, I was afraid.

We are all scared to death of death. We seem to know so little about it, yet we're all kind of fascinated by it. It's a reality that is going to consume us and all of our loved ones sooner or later. Though we might not obsess about it, it's a reality that hovers in the background of our minds.

One movie that tapped into our fascination with and fear of death was *The Sixth Sense* (1999). The movie made the cover of numerous magazines and raised the topic of what happens when we die. For a while, everyone was talking about this movie. Who could forget the kid's immortal, so to speak, line: "I see dead people"?

BEING RATIONAL ABOUT DEATH

Hollywood and TV are filled with all sorts of spooky films about death. This may help explain why we aren't all that rational when it comes to death. If we were rational about it, we'd realise that if death is all there is, it nullifies everything about life and makes it all meaningless.

Well-known British author, professor and parliamentarian Bryan Magee wrote about just how great his life was going. By any standard, he had it all—and then some:

"No doubt," he wrote, "on the surface I seemed to have everything I could reasonably want—good health, energy, an adventurous life, rewarding friendships, exhilarating love affairs, success in my work, exciting travel, the sustained nourishment of music, theatre, reading."

However, as he explained it, one little problem arose that threw a damper over the whole thing:

> But in the middle of it all I was overwhelmed, almost literally so, by a sense of mortality. The realisation hit me like a demolition crane that I was inevitably going to die. . . . Death, my death, the literal destruction of me, was totally inevitable, and had been from the very instant of my conception. Nothing that I could ever do, now or at any other time, could make any difference to that, nor could it ever have done so at any moment in my life.

The conclusions he drew about the reality of death were less than comforting:

> In the eyes of eternity a human lifespan is barely a flicker. Death will be upon us before we know where we are; and once we are dead it will be forever. What

can anything I do mean or matter to me when I have gone down into complete nothingness for the rest of eternity? What can it matter to anyone else, either, when they too are eternally nothing? If the void is the permanent destination of all of us, all value and all significance are merely pretended for the purpose of carrying on our little human game, like children dressing up.

In the end, he realised that no matter what he accomplished, "none of it would make the slightest difference to me or to anyone else when all of us were nothing, as everyone was going to be, including everyone not yet born; that it could therefore make no difference when I died, and would have made no difference if I had never been born; that I was in any event going to be for all eternity what I would have been if I had never been born; that there was no meaning in any of it, no point in any of it; and that in the end everything was nothing."

Magee's not the only one to draw these conclusions. Centuries ago, there lived a French writer, mathematician, physicist, inventor and Catholic philosopher named Blaise Pascal. He was a child prodigy, even inventing what is considered the world's first computer while still a teenager. No wonder, then, that one of the earlier computer languages developed in the 20th century was named after him. He was a rare genius with some brilliant insights on death.

First, he wrote about the certainty of death. He wrote that there is no real "lasting satisfaction" in life and that "death, which threatens us every moment" is going to last forever. No matter how long we live here, what follows is going to be a lot longer. The only logical and reasonable thing to do is find out what happens after death because whatever it is, it's going to last a lot longer than life.

"For it is not to be doubted," wrote Pascal, "that the duration of this life is but a moment; that the state of death is eternal, whatever may be its nature; and that thus all our actions and thoughts must take such different directions according to the state of that eternity. . . . There is nothing more clearer than this."

He was appalled by the irrationality of those "who live without thought of the ultimate end of life, who let themselves be guided by their own inclinations and pleasures without reflection and without concern, and, as if they could annihilate eternity by turning away their thoughts from it, think only of making themselves happy for the moment."

Suppose you were 21 years old, or 40 or 64 and in good health, too. Suppose someone came up to you and said, "Look, I have special powers and can give you whatever you want for yourself. Beauty, riches, happiness, fame, love, whatever—you can have it all. There's only one catch: after two years, you will die."

What rational and logical person would accept such a deal? This is exactly what Pascal is saying. The difference is that very few of us get what we want in this life. We die after a relatively short time anyway so what does it matter?

The only sensible thing would be for us to find out, if possible, what death is all about. What does it mean and what do we face when we die? It's a reasonable question since we're going to be in that state a lot longer than the state we find ourselves in now.

THE QUESTION OF DEATH

This leads to perhaps the greatest question, the greatest mystery and the greatest dilemma that humans face: the question of death. Some would argue that you can't answer the most basic questions about life until you can answer the most basic questions about death.

So what is death all about? What happens at death and is it forever? Is there something beyond and if so, what is it? Is Pascal's logic right in saying that no matter how long we live in this life, what comes after will be a whole lot longer? As long as human beings have lived and died, they have struggled with understanding death. There's an incredible array of views available regarding what happens at death.

For example, consider the iconic pyramids of Egypt. These were tombs for the Pharaohs, built especially for the dead. As with all the ancient cultures, the Egyptians had elaborate belief systems about people heading off to another existence after they died. There seems to be as many different concepts of what happens to the dead as there are religions, cults and philosophies. In some ancient cultures, things like food, water, furniture, and even slaves and wives were placed in the tombs with the dead. They firmly believed the dead would need them in the afterlife.

The ancient Greek concept of the afterlife was depicted by the poet Homer. He often described the Underworld, deep beneath the earth. In a place called Hades, the being by that name who was brother to Zeus and Poseidon, and his wife, Persephone, reigned over an endless number of unfortunate souls. They were called "the shades"—people who had died and ended up there. The ghost of the great warrior Achilles told Odysseus that he would rather be a poor serf on earth than lord of all the dead in the Underworld.

There are all sorts of beliefs about reincarnation, which is the idea that you assume another body in another life when you die. Depending on how you lived your life, you might return as the great king of a vast and wealthy empire. On the other hand, you might return as a hungry dog sniffing through waste bins in a Calcutta slum in India.

A philosopher from the 17th century, Rene Descartes—known most famously for his line, "I think, therefore I am"—believed the immortal soul was lodged in the pineal gland, a small endocrine gland in the brain. Here was the place, he theorised, where the physical body and the non-physical soul somehow interacted with each other.

There are also various beliefs in Christianity and Judaism about the fate of the dead. There are many views about where they go, as well as the existence of heaven, hell, purgatory and the like—views about as widely divergent as there are different groups of Jews and Christians.

SECULAR DEATH

And now a scientific element has added a new argument—the science of "near-death experiences" (NDEs). So many stories and books have come out about people who, having been "clinically dead," come back and tell incredible stories. Even scientists are studying this phenomenon because so many of them feature a visit to another realm. Thus, NDEs have taken on a veneer of science. In many minds, this gives them greater status and credibility.

Yet we should be cautious when considering these stories. They're not called near-death experiences for nothing. They're only near death and just being near something isn't the same as actually experiencing it. To be "near" death isn't the same as being dead, any more than being near birth is to be born. None of the people who have had these experiences have been dead, as in rigor mortis dead, so we need to be careful about the conclusions we draw.

Even though these stories come wrapped in science, what happens to the dead may have nothing to do with what these experiences are about. Just as we can't learn much about cirrhosis of the liver from looking at a beer commercial, drawing too many conclusions about death from near death experiences is flawed.

Of course, not everyone believes in the afterlife. An ancient Roman writer, Titus Lucretius Carus, wrote a six-book long poem called *On the Nature of the Universe*, in which he gave compelling arguments against the immortality of the soul (mostly in Book 3).

Today, particularly in secular cultures, many believe that death is the end. You live, you die and your life is over when your heart stops beating. There's nothing else—you just decompose into the nothingness out of which you first came.

A good example is someone like Richard Dawkins. In a compilation of essays, he wrote about the death of a fellow evolutionary biologist, D W Hamilton. Dawkins talked about Hamilton's desire for his corpse to be interred in the Amazon jungle with a bunch of beetles, which he apparently liked to study.

Dawkins quoted the eulogy of Hamilton's wife at the funeral, which took place not in the Amazon, as he had wanted, but in England. Farewelling her husband, she said:

> Bill, now your body is lying in the Wytham woods, but from here you will reach again your beloved forests. You will live not only in a beetle, but in billions of spores of fungi and algae. Brought by the wind higher up in the troposphere, all of you will form the clouds, and wandering across oceans, will fall down and fly up again and again, till eventually a drop of rain will join you to the water of the flooded forest of the Amazon.

With all due respect, this isn't the most thrilling of prospects. It's just not the most glorious of endings to a human's existence. Who wants to float around in spores of fungi and algae? Is that all we have to look forward to when we go? Dawkins ended his eulogy for Hamilton with a line from Wordsworth, ". . . a mind forever/ Voyaging through strange seas of thought, alone."

Hamilton died at the age of 68, and whichever parts of him floated among the "spores of fungi and algae," it certainly wasn't his mind living forever. As we understand it, Dawkins's words were corny and goofy sentimental kitsch—nothing more.

But if we do not believe in the supernatural or anything other than "atoms and the void," as one ancient Greek philosopher put it, what else is there?

DEATH IN THE BIBLE

So what does the Bible have to say about death? This book has explored biblical perspectives on a number of crucial issues, including morality, the rise of evil, the law of God and the search for truth. It would be surprising if the Bible didn't address one of the biggest questions humanity faces.

There are two overarching views in Christianity about death, as well as what we might do in this life to prepare for whatever comes next.

The most popular and widely-believed view by far is that the person goes off to his or her reward or punishment immediately after death. The choices here are heaven or hell—or in some cases, purgatory. Some Pentecostal churches even call the burial preparation for its members "homegoings."

This is the common view in most non-Christian religions, in one form or another. What they might differ on is where you go, what it's like when you get there or why you go where you do. Even so, the common view is that something goes on living, consciously, right after death. In other words, you don't really die. Instead, you enter another realm of existence.

Though it has a long history, there is another view that is much less common. This view, still believed by many Christians, is that the dead are asleep and remain that way until the end of time. At that point, Jesus will return to resurrect the faithful to eternal life in new bodies.

These are two very different views. Either the dead are asleep, unconscious and oblivious to everything, or they're in the bliss of heaven or, as the case may be, the torture of hell. Or perhaps they are in some conscious state in between.

We need to know which is true—the answer is important to all of us. After all, think of how much it affects our life and our stories. No matter who we are, we all know how our story is going to end. We might not know the particular time, place and circumstance but our story is going to end just like everyone else's—in some hole in the ground or in an urn.

We really want to get this one right.

As you look over a few Bible texts, think about the question: Do these texts make sense if, as is commonly believed, the dead go soaring off immediately to some other conscious state in another realm of existence? Do the texts make better sense if the dead sleep, unconsciously, in the grave until the Second Coming when they are resurrected and given new physical bodies?

Here's Jesus Himself, talking about the dead:

> Do not marvel at this; for the hour is coming in which all who are in the graves will hear His voice and come forth—those who have done good, to the resurrection of life, and those who have done evil, to the resurrection of condemnation (John 5:28, 29).

Does this sound like the dead have gone to their reward or punishment as soon as they died? It sounds more like they are in the grave, awaiting some kind of end-time judgment. Which view makes the most sense here?

Think about it, then note the words of this text:

And many of those who sleep in the dust of the earth shall awake, some to everlasting life, some to shame and everlasting contempt (Daniel 12:2).

If the dead are already being rewarded or punished as soon as they die, how can they also be asleep in the dust of the earth? Also note that both those who face everlasting life and those facing everlasting contempt are in the same place until they awake.

Psalm 6:5 states, "For in death there is no remembrance of You; in the grave who will give You thanks?" In response to those who denied the resurrection of the dead, Paul wrote:

And if Christ is not risen, your faith is futile; you are still in your sins! Then also those who have fallen asleep in Christ have perished (1 Corinthians 15:17, 18).

What does it mean if those "fallen asleep"—Jesus used the same term to describe the death of His friend Lazarus (see John 11:11–14)—in Christ are lost if there's no resurrection? If the dead in Christ are already in heaven, this doesn't make sense. If, however, the dead are asleep and unconscious in the grave, the texts make better sense.

Jesus spoke specifically about His return when He said: "And behold, I am coming quickly, and My reward is with Me, to give to every one according to his work" (Revelation 22:12).

Don't those who have died faithful to Jesus get their reward as soon as they die, soaring off to heaven? Isn't that what's commonly taught and believed? As many of Christ's faithful followers have been dead for centuries, when do they get their reward? Certainly they should have been enjoying it long before now, rather than waiting for Jesus' return.

But Jesus is saying that the reward comes with Him. If His faithful followers are dead, asleep and knowing nothing, the words make sense. The dead are dead, and only when Jesus returns and raises them will they get their reward.

This is the grand rescue we talked about earlier!

Look at the following texts about death and think about what they mean if the deceased are in heaven or hell:

- "His spirit departs, he returns to his earth; in that very day his plans perish" (Psalm 146:4).
- "The dead do not praise the Lord, nor any who go down into silence" (Psalm 115:17).
- "For the living know that they will die; but the dead know nothing" (Ecclesiastes 9:5).

Again, what do these texts mean if the dead go off to some immediate reward or punishment as soon as they die? It makes no sense at all.

What does make sense is that death is an unconscious sleep and the dead know nothing. They stay that way until the end of time, when there is a resurrection and a judgment.

THE GREAT CONTROVERSY MOTIF

So why is there so much confusion on this topic, even among Christians?

Remember that we are in the middle of a great controversy between Christ and Satan—between good and evil. If you were the devil and you didn't want people to believe in Jesus, the easiest way to do so is by giving them all sorts of beliefs about an afterlife that doesn't require Jesus. You would have them believe there's something inherently immortal about themselves that will live on forever, whether they believe in Jesus or not.

Of course, this leads to one big question: if all the dead sleep until the end, what about judgment? If all the dead are asleep, Adolph Hitler is now in the same place as Anne Frank. Some of the world's most gruesome killers are in the same place as those they killed.

That's not a very good kind of justice, unless there is eventually some kind of final reckoning.

Or, worse, if there is some kind of final reckoning, what if we're cast into the eternal burning hellfire? What kind of justice is that? If that was justice, it would be better for all the dead to stay dead. No final punishment for evil at all would be better than people being punished in an eternally burning hell! We're going to look at the whole question of God's justice, judgment and punishment in the next chapter. They tell us a lot about what God is really like. And the answers are full of surprises—and good ones, too.

There's a funny story told about Albert Einstein as a forgetful old man. He was on a train and the conductor asked him for his ticket. Einstein reached into one pocket, then another and another, and couldn't find the ticket.

"Don't worry, Dr Einstein," the conductor said. "I know who you are. We all know who you are. I'm sure you bought the ticket." The conductor then moved on to the next car in the train. But before he reached the next car, he looked back and saw Einstein down on his hands and knees, looking under the seat for his ticket.

The conductor rushed back and said, "Dr Einstein, Dr Einstein, don't worry. I know who you are. Don't worry about the ticket. I'm sure you bought one."

Einstein looked up and said, "Young man, I know who I am, too. What I don't know is where I am going."

Maybe we know who we are—or are at least are in the process of learning—but the deeper question is where we are going. As we've said before, we're all part of the larger epic playing out around us. At least in our own little part of the story, we're the stars.

Our story begins with our life here, which is important to us. It's all we have for now, so what we do and how we live now matters.

But if our journey eternally ends when our life on earth does, it's a pretty short jaunt. For many, it's a pretty bitter trip, too. If that's all there is, we could argue that what we do here doesn't matter at all in the grand scheme of things.

That's why we need to know, and why the poet W H Auden wrote:

> Nothing can save us that is possible;
> We who must die demand a miracle.

Many believe—and with good reason, too—such a miracle is found in Jesus.

hell's **bell**

Writer P J O' Rourke, known for his outrageous and bawdy sense of humour, once wrote a book called—and I;ll give you its full title—*Holidays in Hell: In Which Our Intrepid Reporter Travels to the World's Worst Places and Asks, "What's Funny About This?"*

There are some places that can aptly be described as "hell on earth," even though the phrase is nothing more than a metaphor. But there is a literal hell on earth—it's located about 100 kilometres (60 miles) south of Detroit.

The real hell is Hell, Michigan, with a population of around 266. The United States postal code of Hell is 48169. And, in case you were wondering, Hell's coordinates are 42°26'05"N 83°59'06"W.

When visiting Hell, the Screams Ice Cream Parlour is a nice place to stop in on those hot days in Hell.

Just down the road is Hell in a Handbasket general store, formerly known as Hell Country Store and Spirits. How apt to have spirits in Hell.

How does a pleasant little town get stuck with a name like "Hell"?

There are two stories about it that have been circulating for years now.

The first one says that a pair of German travellers stepped out of a stagecoach one sunny afternoon in the 1830s. One said to the other, "So schön hell!" which translates as "So beautifully bright!" Some locals overheard their comments and the name stuck.

The second goes like this: after Michigan gained statehood, George Reeves, a New York farmer who started some small businesses in the 1830s that eventually turned into a minor town, was asked what he thought the town he helped settle should be called. According to the story, he replied, "You can name it Hell for all I care."

The name became official on October 13, 1841.

Hell gets a lot of mileage out of the name, too. It sponsors a running event called "Run Thru Hell," which includes 16-kilometre (10-mile) and 8-kilometre (4.8-mile) races. Proud participants receive a T-shirt that reads, "I Ran Thru Hell."

The Ann Arbor Bicycle Touring Society also hosts an annual recreational event called "One Helluva Ride."

The inhabitants of Hell clearly enjoy the irony of their town's name.

A LITTLE HISTORY OF HELL

In one sense, it's very silly. If Hell, Michigan, were named Jonesburg or Sykesville, it would be just another small town. But because the word "hell" is so fully of imagery, meaning and emotion, any place named "Hell" is going to get our attention.

It's understandable when all of us have heard preachers on TV, the radio or online warn about the eternal fires of hell. In fact, you can watch a YouTube clip of what is said to be the screams of people burning in hell right now.

Hard as it might be to believe, the internet has various stories about some miners drilling in Siberia when, much to their surprise, they started to hear the sounds of people screaming in pain.

The weird thing is some people honestly think this is true—or could be true. They honestly believe there is a hole in the earth where people are being tormented in "fire and brimstone." Though this story is being debated as a hoax, the fact that anyone would take it seriously shows the fascination many people have with hell.

The 14th-century poet, Dante Alighieri, is responsible for creating the most famous and enduring depiction of eternal torment and suffering in hell. His famous epic poem *The Divine Comedy* begins with a section called "Inferno," the Italian word for "hell." It tells of the Roman poet, Virgil, guiding Dante through the wretched place.

In the poem, hell is said to consist of nine circles that go deeper and deeper under the earth as the torments of the unfortunate souls there get worse and worse. Which circle a person wound up in was said to depend, of course, on how much they sinned while on earth.

The most famous part of the poem is the beginning, at the entrance of hell. As Dante and Virgil reach it, there is a sign that reads "Abandon all hope, ye who enter here."

The sad thing is that though this poem is pure fiction, it's hard to underestimate how influential it has been. Through the centuries, it has helped form the common idea of hell.

In *A Portrait of the Artist as a Young Man*, Irish novelist and poet James Joyce explains how hell was described to him when he was a child. Here, a priest explains:

> Hell is a strait and dark and foul-smelling prison, an abode of demons and lost souls, filled with fire and smoke. The straitness of this prison house is expressly designed by God to punish those who refused to be bound by His laws. . . .

The torment of fire is the greatest torment to which the tyrant has ever subjected his fellow creatures. Place your finger for a moment in the flame of a candle and you will feel the pain of fire. But our earthly fire was created by God for the benefit of man, to maintain in him the spark of life and to help him in the useful arts, whereas the fire of hell is of another quality and was created by God to torture and punish the unrepentant sinner. . . .

You have often seen the sand on the seashore. How fine are its tiny grains! And how many of those tiny little grains go to make up the small handful which a child grasps in its play. Now imagine a mountain of that sand, a million miles high, reaching from the earth to the farthest heavens, and a million miles broad, extending to remotest space, and a million miles in thickness; and imagine such an enormous mass of countless particles of sand multiplied as often as there are leaves in the forest, drops of water in the mighty ocean, feathers on birds, scales on fish, hairs on animals, atoms in the vast expanse of the air: and imagine that at the end of every million years a little bird came to that mountain and carried away in its beak a tiny grain of that sand. How many millions upon millions of centuries would pass before that bird had carried away even a square foot of that mountain, how many eons upon eons of ages before it had carried away all? Yet at the end of that immense stretch of time not even one instant of eternity could be said to have ended. At the end of all those billions and trillions of years eternity would have scarcely begun.

Obviously, Joyce was mocking the whole concept of hell and how the clergy would use it to frighten the students into submission.

French writer Jean-Paul Sartre wrote a play about hell, called *No Exit*. It involved two women and a man locked together in a room and has been made into a film on several occasions. This depiction of hell is nothing like what Joyce or even Dante wrote about. There are no flames, no fire and no devil with a pitchfork. Instead, the idea is that these three people are perfectly suited to make each other miserable for all eternity—and that's just what they do.

One of Sartre's most famous lines come from this play: "Hell—is other people."

Whether you believe in hell or not—or whatever you might think it is, if you do—there's no question that the concept looms large in the human mind.

WHAT THE HELL?

Perhaps there's a reason that people think on the concept of hell a lot.

As we have already noted, one of the certain facts of life is death. It's not a new idea that whatever happens after we die is going to last a lot longer than how long we have lived here.

Whatever hell is, people think it's one of the two inevitable places we could go at death. It would be strange not to think about it when the idea of hell, or some kind of immediate punishment at death, has been part of our thinking for so much of human history.

If you have a guilty conscience about how you have lived—if there's a little pricking in the back of your mind about what you might face "on the other side"—it makes sense that you would have an interest in knowing more.

But as we saw in the previous chapter, there's a great deal of misconception about death itself. The Bible is pretty clear—death is an unconscious sleep. If you believe the Bible, you're safe from so many of the delusions, tricks and outright supernatural deceptions the world is caught up in.

Don't forget that we are all part of the great controversy between Christ and Satan. In this context, it is especially pertinent: "So the great dragon was cast out, that serpent of old, called the Devil and Satan, who deceives the whole world" (Revelation 12:9).

If what we're discovering about death is correct—that it is an unconscious sleep—then much of the world is being deceived, just as the text says. They are being misled because they follow what the majority believes about death.

On one level, it all makes sense. The dead being asleep seems reasonable and biblical, despite popular misconceptions like those portrayed in Dante's *Divine Comedy*.

THE JUSTICE THING

But on another level, it leads to a big problem. As we mentioned in the previous chapter, is it fair for everyone to go to the same grave in an unconscious sleep? That would mean that Mao Tse-Tung—under whose reign an estimated 70 million people died, including about 38 million in a famine his government helped create—died comfortably and peaceably, and is now resting in the same place as many of his innocent victims. Obviously, this includes the Christians he had murdered.

It's logical to question the justice of a God who would burn sinful people in hell for all eternity. The image of God as the Eternal Torturer doesn't exactly give us confidence in trusting Him. It wouldn't be justice at all.

But as bad as that is—and that is bad—what if there were no final judgment at all? What if all the evil and good went unpunished or unrewarded? What if the only justice this world ever saw happened in this life alone?

That would hardly be justice, either. In a book called *The Devil's Delusion: Atheism and Its Scientific Pretensions*, David Berlinski wrote about the early days of the Nazi advance into Eastern Europe:

> Before the possibility of Soviet retribution even entered their troubled imagination, Nazi extermination squads would sweep into villages, and after forcing villagers to dig their own graves, murder their victims with machine guns. On one such occasion somewhere in Eastern Europe, an SS officer watched languidly, his machine gun cradled, as an elderly and bearded Hasidic Jew laboriously dug what he knew to be his grave.
>
> Standing straight up, he addressed his executioner. "God is watching what you are doing," he said.

And then he was shot dead. Obviously, that SS officer didn't care that God was watching. Maybe he didn't think God would care about what he was doing, even if God was watching. Whatever the reason, the SS officer wasn't concerned about answering for his actions one day.

So is this act of cold-blooded evil—and one hundred billion other examples like it—going to be avenged? Or if the word "avenged" is troublesome, will there be some kind of final divine tribunal to deliver the justice painfully lacking in this world?

One thing most everyone can agree on is this: If justice is ever going to be done, there has to be some kind of afterlife. There has to be some kind of existence after this life, because the justice we long for isn't happening in this one.

But just because the dead are asleep, it doesn't mean they are gone forever. Just because divine justice doesn't happen right after death doesn't mean it won't.

On the contrary, the Bible is clear that a time of justice and judgment will come. Notice the future tense—it will come. It may not be here or now, and it's not as soon as people die but justice and judgment must come. To be just, God will bring the justice we sorely lack here when He returns.

In the previous chapter, we looked at some Bible verses, many of which mentioned some kind of future reward or punishment. For example, there will be those "who shall awake, some to everlasting life, some to shame and everlasting contempt" (Daniel 12:2).

At some point in the future, there will be a final reckoning. Justice will be done by God, not by humans and their faulty, corrupted courts of law. Who else but the One who knows everything—all thoughts and motives—could be our judge? "For God will bring every work into judgment, including every secret thing, whether good or evil" (Ecclesiastes 12:14).

That's a straightforward promise of judgment and justice from the Bible. Every work, every secret thing that you do—whether good or evil—will be brought to judgment.

THE PINTO

Some people mock the idea of a future judgment because, they say, it has been used by power elites to keep the masses in line. The poor were admonished with something like: Don't worry about reward or punishments now. It will all come later, in God's final judgment, so just accept your hard lot in this life as God's will and wait for the promise of heaven.

This is probably what Karl Marx had in mind when he called religion "the opium of the people." It's true that it has been abused in the past and still is today.

Think, for instance, of the young people who become suicide bombers, told over and over that they are going to be immediately rewarded in their version of heaven. That's abuse of the concept but it doesn't make the idea itself wrong. That would be like saying using the internet to look up child pornography somehow makes it invalid for every other purpose.

Deep down we know that the only hope we have for justice being done is if God does it. He's the only hope we have because if God isn't going to do it, we may as well give up. Forget it—there is no justice and never will be without Him.

Back in the 1970s, the notorious Ford Pinto was rushed into production. It soon became apparent that this horrible little car created in Detroit was dangerous. In a rear-end collision, the fuel tank could explode and kill or seriously burn the passengers.

The bigwigs at Ford—including the famous Lee Iacocca—did a little maths, estimating the number of people who would be killed or maimed by these gas tank explosions each year. They then calculated how much each lawsuit would cost them for those deaths and injuries, in contrast to what it would cost them to fix the problem.

Because it was cheaper to pay the lawsuits, Ford decided to leave the car as it was.

In other words, Ford was willing to let people get killed or burned because it was cheaper than fixing the car!

Back in the 1970s when the world was just learning about the danger of Pintos, one article read:

> A woman, whom for legal reasons we will call Sandra Gillespie, pulled onto a Minneapolis highway in her new Ford Pinto. Riding with her was a young boy, whom we'll call Robbie Carlton. As she entered a merge lane, Sandra Gillespie's car stalled. Another car rear-ended hers at a speed of 28 miles per hour. The Pinto's gas tank ruptured. Vapours from it mixed quickly with the air in the passenger compartment. A spark ignited the mixture and the car exploded in a ball of fire. Sandra died in agony a few hours later in an emergency hospital. Her passenger, 13-year-old Robbie Carlton, is still alive; he has just come home from another futile operation aimed at grafting a new ear and nose from skin on the few unscarred portions of his badly burned body.

Meanwhile, Iacocca has long ago retired and lives in the lap of luxury. No-one has ever been punished for this great injustice. This is why we need the promise of justice and judgment found over and over again in the Bible, to reassure us that it will come one day.

THE FIRES OF HELL

But this leads us back to the topic we started with: hell.

The Bible does talk about hell, final punishment and hellfire. It's biblical and it's real—it's just not burning eternally.

The idea became muddled and confused when the ancient Greek concept of the immortal soul got mingled with biblical religion. The Bible does not teach the concept of an immortal soul.

Yes, there is going to be a final judgment and a final punishment. The Bible is clear: the justice that has not happened here will be administered one day. Mao, Hitler and others will likely get their just desserts. God will judge each of us according to His infinite knowledge. He is the only One who could judge us fairly because He is a God of justice.

But, at the same time, a God of justice could not burn people in hell for all eternity. What kind of justice would that be? We'd be better off with no final judgment than one that included eternal torment.

Sammy "the Bull" Gravano was a mobster tied in with the infamous John Gotti, also known as the "Teflon Don" because he kept getting acquitted. Every time crime-fighting agencies in the United States threw charges at him, he somehow escaped being found guilty. He was only put away after Gravano turned state's witness and testified against him.

As a young man, Gravano was being initiated into the Mafia. He was in a back room with some other mobsters when one of them, named Paul, grabbed his hand and pinched his trigger finger so hard that blood spurted out. He then took Gravano's finger and held it over a "holy" card of a Roman Catholic saint. Someone then set fire to the card while Paul held Gravano's bleeding finger over the flame. "Honour the oath," he said. "If you divulge any of the secrets of this society, your soul will burn like this saint."

While Gravano didn't honour the oath, there's something worth noting about this initiation ritual. He was warned that if he divulged any of the secrets, his soul would burn like the card of that saint. Whatever Paul had in mind for Gravano's soul, that "holy" card only burnt until the paper was consumed. Because it was destroyed, it perished in the fire. This means it could not burn forever.

One of the most famous texts in the entire Bible reads:

> For God so loved the world that He gave His only begotten Son, that whoever believes in Him should not perish but have everlasting life (John 3:16).

There are two fates presented in this verse. One is the promise of "everlasting life," which is contrasted with the only other option. It does not say whoever believes in him should not "burn in eternal fire forever and ever." Instead, the verse says "perish." This means being completely destroyed—gone forever. It's the same as that card, consumed forever in the flames under Gravano's finger.

Hell is real and the punishment is real. The fire is real as well, it's just not eternal. People are destroyed in hell—not eternally tormented there.

Look at the words of Jesus: "And do not fear those who kill the body but cannot kill the soul. But rather fear Him who is able to destroy both soul and body in hell" (Matthew 10:28). If ever a Bible verse proved the soul isn't immortal or that hell wasn't eternal, this is it. Those who face hell are destroyed but that is not the same as eternal torment.

Consider how Paul describes it:

> These shall be punished with everlasting destruction from the presence of the
> Lord and from the glory of His power (2 Thessalonians 1:9).

The end result is everlasting and eternal. This means the destruction is eternal, not the act of destroying.

The difference is very important. We know that our God of justice will bring judgment on this world and evil will be recompensed. But what a difference knowing God will destroy evil once and for all, rather than this idea of Him tormenting, burning and torturing people forever in hell.

While there are some texts that talk about eternal fire, we need to understand the language of the Bible and how it is used.

Many have heard the story of Sodom and Gomorrah. In the Bible, they are depicted as pretty bad places. Here's an example of a typical day in Sodom and Gomorrah: A few visitors come to visit the house of a man named Lot, who lived in Sodom. A mob comes to the house and demands that these strangers be brought out so they can gang rape them. Lot pleads with the mob outside his house to be reasonable. God eventually wipes out both Sodom and Gomorrah, completely destroying them with fire. They are no more—gone.

With this in mind, look at a text from the New Testament:

> As Sodom and Gomorrah, and the cities around them in a similar manner to these,
> having given themselves over to sexual immorality and gone after strange flesh, are
> set forth as an example, suffering the vengeance of eternal fire (Jude 1:7).

As these places aren't still burning, we need to rethink our understanding of "eternal" fire. Both were completely destroyed and to this day, archaeologists dispute their location. If an eternal fire was still burning, they would be easy to find.

In this context, "eternal" means completed, fulfilled and accomplished forever. This is just the kind of language the Bible uses.

When the Bible talks about God bringing judgment on a place, such as Jerusalem, it talks about him destroying the place with a fire that shall "burn and not be quenched" (see Jeremiah 7:20). D

oes this mean the fire is still burning somewhere today? It's safe to say there's no eternally burning fire in these places. Instead, it's biblical language that gives the idea of completion—that the fire will do its work and nothing can stop it.

Think about what this says about the character of God. If God is a God of justice, justice will be done. Evil will be destroyed forever and the destruction of evil will be everlasting. Everything that is sinful will be gone forever.

There's no hole in the ground where people are tormented forever, as commonly taught. The God of the Bible would not do that.

What a tragedy that this idea of an eternal, burning hell continues to be preached and promoted.

A RETURN TO THE VOID

All human beings have one powerful thing in common: we didn't ask to be born. All of us were born into this world without our own consent.

We had no choice in the matter whatsoever.

It's like we came out of nothingness. We don't exist, then there we are as an egg and a sperm. United, they begin the process that resulted in each of us. But separated, a sperm and an egg do not make a person. Before that moment of conception, we were nothing.

Of course, God knows this. I believe God is offering us one of two alternatives:

We can have the eternal life He originally wanted for us or we can go back to what we were before we were conceived—nothing.

It's all there in John 3:16.

It presents the two opposites: everlasting life, offered to us all in Jesus, or nothingness. We didn't choose to exist and we don't have to, not if we don't want it. God will respect that choice.

In the end, that's what judgment is about, at least partially: God respecting our choice, one way or another.

It's up to us to make the choice that will last us for the rest of forever: eternal life or eternal nothingness?

Unlike some of the more recent and horrific natural disasters, no-one could say they had no warning.

For months, scientists and seismologists were expressing concern that Mount St Helens, in Washington State, USA, was showing increasing activity. Of course, this was nothing new. As far back as the late 1700s, explorers, traders and missionaries had heard reports about it erupting. Indeed, throughout the 1800s and even in the early 1900s, the mountain had been the source of lava flows, eruptions, earthquakes and spewing ash.

By the time of the infamous eruption in 1980, people knew it was coming—and coming soon. They just didn't know when.

After a five-year period in which the mountain had 44 earthquakes, around March 15, 1980, Mount St Helens had a week where more than 100 were recorded. On March 20, a magnitude 4.2 quake triggered avalanches on the mountain. The next day, seismologists suspected the mountain was about to have its first eruption since 1857. They just weren't ready to make it public, in case they were wrong.

On May 18, at about 8:30 in the morning, the north face of the volcano slid away in a landslide, causing the rest to explode—the most deadly and economically-damaging volcanic eruption in American history. By the time it was over, the St Helens eruption killed 57 people, destroyed 250 homes, wiped out 47 bridges, 24 kilometres (15 miles) of railway lines and almost 300 kilometres (185 miles) of highway.

The explosion itself released 24 megatons of thermal energy—1,600 times the size of the atomic bomb dropped on Hiroshima! A shockwave travelled horizontally over the area at speeds of more than 1000 kilometres per hour (above 670 miles per hour). Flows of gas and rock, which reached up to about 400°C (800°F), raced down the mountain at more than 300 kilometres per hour (200 miles per hour). Everything in the direct blast zone, natural or manmade, was obliterated within seconds. Nothing could deflect the force of the blast—it just took out everything.

There was devastation—burned trees and the like—as far as almost 30 kilometres (19 miles) away. On that same day, winds blew more than 500 million tons of ash eastward and caused complete darkness in Spokane, Washington, 400 kilometres (250 miles) from the volcano.

Nothing like it had ever occurred in the United States. As far as volcanic activity went, the world hadn't seen anything like it in many years.

And, as we said, you can't say people weren't warned.

THE DIVING BELL AND THE BUTTERFLY

Of course, it's easy to give a warning. Heeding that warning is another thing altogether. After all, look at all the warnings on packets of cigarettes about what smoking can do to you. Even with pictures of lung cancer, heart disease, emphysema and the like, people still start smoking. What good is a warning if people take no notice of it?

With the Mount St Helens eruption, there's the famous story of the crotchety old man who had lived for 54 years near the base of Mount St Helens. With rather salty language, he told the authorities he wasn't leaving, despite being warned about what was coming. And, true to his word, he didn't leave.

He's still there today, squashed under tons of ash and water.

What a contrast to the story of Jean-Dominique Bauby. Bauby was a well-known French journalist and author. He was also editor in chief of *Elle*, the elite French fashion magazine. He was at the top of his game and had it all—and then some.

Then, without any warning to indicate what was coming, he had a massive stroke. Just like that on December 8, 1995, he lost the ability to do anything. He was 43 years old.

When he woke 20 days later, he was unable to talk. His body was paralysed and all he could do was blink his left eyelid. His condition is called "locked-in syndrome" and it means that, though the mental faculties remain intact, the body is paralysed.

In Bauby's case, his mouth, arms and legs were paralysed, and he lost 27 kilograms (60 pounds) in the first 20 weeks after his stroke. What was amazing was that he managed to use the only part of his body he could still control, his left eye, to dictate a book.

The book became the bestseller *The Diving Bell and the Butterfly*, which was made into a movie starring Mathieu Amalric as Bauby. The movie won awards at the Cannes Film Festival and the Golden Globes, and even got four Academy Award nominations.

Next time you feel sorry for yourself, think of this one line from the book:

> But for now, I would be the happiest of men if I could just swallow the overflow of saliva that endlessly floods my mouth.

There was no warning and no indication—not anything.

Just like that, everything can change.

WOE TO THE INHABITANTS!

Things can come upon us in the most unexpected ways. At times we have warning, as with Mount St Helens. Other times, as with Bauby, we have no warning at all.

Although we have touched on a lot of good news amid the darkness of our world, this book is also a warning. We are in the midst of a great controversy between good and evil, and we have to choose which side of this battle we are on.

There's one text in particular that we have looked at again and again, which is nothing if not a warning:

> Therefore rejoice, O heavens, and you who dwell in them! Woe to the inhabitants of the earth and the sea! For the devil has come down to you, having great wrath, because he knows that he has a short time (Revelation 12:12).

"Woe to the inhabitants of the earth and the sea" definitely sounds like a warning. Also note that it says the devil's time is short. From our perspective, century upon century of human history doesn't seem that short. But as we have explored, there is a greater, grander perspective of the world and the universe. There's a greater reality out there than what we can see, comprehend or experience.

However, when this text says the devil's time is short, it means one thing for sure: sooner or later, it will all be over. The great rescue is going to happen and this broken mess of life on earth, as it now exists, is going to be finished.

And, as we now understand, we have to be on one side or the other—there is no middle ground.

There was no middle ground on the Titanic—you either survived or you died.

It's the same for the great controversy. We're part of this bigger story, though much of the background of our own stories wasn't our own choosing. We make choices within the confines and limits of the background we have been given—choices that place us on one side or the other.

There are experimental theatres in which the actors, placed on the stage with certain props, improvise as they go along. They don't have a script to follow—each has to make their own choices.

And we have to do the same thing with ourselves. But, unlike those on the stage, it isn't so easy to walk away from the choices we make in life. Some still do—it's what we call "suicide."

Among the choices we have to make is whether we heed the warnings we are given.

THE FIRST ANGEL

Do you want to know how this great controversy is going to end before it does?

All you have to do is read the last few chapters of the Bible. They paint a wonderful picture of the future, portraying a reality vastly different to the one we live in now.

But before that end comes, there's going to be a climactic showdown. As in all battles, there has to be a final round—the confrontation that brings it all to a close. And how fair would it be if we were not warned about what was coming?

Remember the movie Jaws, with Roy Scheider? He played the police chief Martin Brody at a summer resort beach called Amity Island, which was being terrorised by the giant white shark.

Brody was pressured into not saying anything about the shark because it would ruin the summer season business. Soon after, Brody is standing on the beach and a woman comes up and slaps him in the face. Her son had been eaten by the shark the day before and she had just learned that though he knew the water was dangerous, he hadn't closed the beach.

But God is not like that. If we need a warning, He will give it to us.

In fact, He has already given us a warning in the Bible's Book of Revelation. It is known as the Three Angels' Messages of Revelation 14, which many believe is the last warning message to this world.

It is both a warning and the final appeal for us to accept the grace, mercy and forgiveness our loving God offers to every one of us.

Imagine this scene: a little girl is standing by the side of the road and two cars come up to her. One has her concerned parents in it, who plead with the child to get in the car and come back to their loving, caring home. In the other car is a violent child molester, who calls out to the girl, offering her sweets and candy if she would only get in the car. The parents plead with her, warning her—"Don't get into that car with that man!"

Sure, it's a warning—one that comes from hearts filled with love. They want to spare their little girl the terrible consequences of what will happen if she gets in the wrong car!

It's a stark contrast and as we've seen all along, we each face the decision in this epic controversy we find ourselves in.

The First Angel's message reads:

Then I saw another angel flying in the midst of heaven, having the everlasting gospel to preach to those who dwell on the earth—to every nation, tribe, tongue, and people—saying with a loud voice, "Fear God and give glory to Him, for the hour of His judgment has come; and worship Him who made heaven and earth, the sea and springs of water" (Revelation 14:6, 7).

There's a lot of information here but it starts with "the everlasting gospel." This is the message of God's mercy, love and grace to all of us.

As we have noted, all of us are guilty. But the good news of the gospel is that we can all be forgiven, pardoned and made right with God right now. This is the "everlasting gospel"—the first message of the first angel.

This message of warning starts out with hope, promise and the answer to the warning itself. It says that the solution is the gospel of Jesus Christ, which gives us all a chance to start over, be forgiven and look toward a wonderful future.

THE PROMISE OF JUSTICE

The warning also talks about the "hour of his judgment." As we mentioned earlier, judgment and justice must come because a just and honourable God could do nothing else. The lack of justice that makes life so unbearable now will end one day. Judgment will come by a perfect judge, who makes no mistakes.

A 19th-century Spanish general named Luis de Narvaez was on his deathbed. A guest asked him if he had made peace with his enemies:

"I have no enemies," he replied stoically.

"You have no enemies?" his surprised guest repeated.

"Yeah," the dying general continued, "I've had them all shot."

According to the Bible, the justice for this and every other wrong doing is coming.

Years ago, the United States was shocked by the story of 17-year-old David Cash, who watched his best friend take a seven-year old girl into the stall of a casino bathroom and attack her. Cash just walked away and did nothing while his friend molested and murdered the little girl. He didn't call the police, didn't call a security guard and didn't try to stop the assault. He just walked away.

The murderer went to jail but Cash was never formally charged with a crime. When asked by the Los Angeles Times why he did nothing to stop this horrific attack, Cash responded, "I'm not going to get upset over someone else's life. I just worry about myself first. I'm not going to lose sleep over somebody else's problems."

There are so many, many things in this world that cry out for the justice it is not seeing now.

THE WORSHIP OF NOTHING

The First Angel's message also says, "Worship Him who made heaven and earth, the sea and springs of water."

We're told to worship God our Creator—to worship the one who made us and everything else in the universe. We've looked at some of these themes in past chapters, especially when we looked at the Sabbath commandment as a memorial to God as the Creator.

It's a reminder not to worship anything else other than the true God.

British theologian and writer N T Wright has reflected:

> One of the primary laws of human life is that you become like what you worship; what's more, you reflect what you worship not only back on the object itself but also outward to the world around. Those who worship money increasingly define themselves in terms of it and increasingly treat other people as creditors, debtors, partners or customers rather than as human beings.

Anything we worship other than God is meaningless, useless and empty. In the Old Testament, people are warned against worshipping useless things. One of the original Hebrew words used to describe just how useless these things were is a word that means "breath" or "nothingness."

It's kind of ironic to consider but have you ever thought about how much nothingness is out there? There's a lot of nothingness out there and the Bible's call to worship the Creator is an appeal to get away from being trapped in this all-pervading nothingness.

We've all heard of the Roman Emperor Nero. His mother, Agrippina, worshipped power. One story goes that when Nero was still a child, his mother took him to some astrologers and asked about his destiny. When she was told that the child would be emperor, the mother was thrilled. Her dreams of power would come true. But then the astrologers added a small caveat: when he became emperor, he would kill her.

You'd think this would have tempered Agrippina's enthusiasm for him getting power. But, no, she responded, "Let him kill me, so long as he rules!"

What an astonishing lust for power!

Due to the strange and often convoluted way the Romans got their emperors, her son ascended to the throne. Nero and his mother only had to "remove" a few rivals to make it happen. Even astrologers sometimes get it right—no doubt with a little demonic help in the great controversy.

As fate would have it, one of his earliest acts as emperor was to kill his mother, mostly because she disapproved of his latest love interest. He first tried to drown her in a boating "accident" but when she survived that, he sent a bunch of thugs over and they hacked her to death.

There are really only two options: the worship of the true God or the worship of nothingness. Each of us has to make that decision for ourselves.

THE SECOND ANGEL

In the First Angel's message, we're told some very important things. We're given the gospel, told about judgment and called to worship the Creator. This sets the foundation for what comes next, the Second Angel's message. Look at what it says:

> And another angel followed, saying, "Babylon is fallen, is fallen, that great city, because she has made all nations drink of the wine of the wrath of her fornication" (Revelation 14:8).

What does "Babylon is fallen" mean? We know for sure that the angel isn't talking about the downfall of Saddam Hussein in the Iraq war or any of the other endless battles in the Middle East. While many TV evangelists seem obsessed with such battles because the location of ancient Babylon was in that area, this isn't what the Bible is talking about.

The New Testament often uses imagery and language from the Old Testament. Babylon was a violent and corrupt religious, political and economic power that ruled the ancient world. So when Revelation talks about Babylon, it's talking about the large, powerful and corrupt religious, political and economic powers that rule the world today.

It says they are going to fall, so it's all going to come crumbling down!

The powers that have polluted our world, oppressed the poor, trampled on our rights and made the world the mess that it is are not going to last. This verse is telling us what we can sense ourselves—the whole corrupted political, economic and religious system of the world is doomed.

It's warning us, "Don't bet on this world's systems. If you do, you are going to lose."

THE THIRD ANGEL

Finally, we come to the Third Angel's message. It says:

> Then a third angel followed them, saying with a loud voice, "If anyone worships the beast and his image, and receives his mark on his forehead or on his hand, he himself shall also drink of the wine of the wrath of God, which is poured out full strength into the cup of His indignation. He shall be tormented with fire and brimstone in the presence of the holy angels and in the presence of the Lamb. And the smoke of their torment ascends forever and ever; and they have no rest day or night, who worship the beast and his image, and whoever receives the mark of his name" (Revelation 14:9–11).

This warning is about as fearsome and intense as you are ever going to get. There's nothing else in the Bible quite like it.

The first point to remember is what we saw earlier: that the New Testament is using language from the Old. This verse is not talking about eternal torment in hell but that the ultimate punishment will be complete and last forever.

Even so, it's still the most fearsome in the entire Bible.

At the end of time, we will have to face the issue of whom or what we worship. The first angel told us to worship the Creator. The third expands on this by talking about those who worship the "beast and his image," or any system or person other than the Lord Himself.

What's crucial, however, is what we have been saying all along—there is no middle ground. The message of the three angels is that each of us has to make a decision. This means either worshipping the Lord or worshipping the beast and his image, the great religious and political systems that rule the world that are contrary to what God and His Word teaches.

Here is where this great battle between good and evil, right and wrong, Christ and Satan ends.

We each have to choose which side to be on, God's side or Satan's side.

So how can we know for sure that we are on God's side? We know the text said that Satan "deceives the whole world" (Revelation 12:9). How can we know, for sure, that we going to wind up on the right side of this cosmic battle?

The answer is found in the next verse, where—in contrast to those who worship the beast and his image—the Bible gives a description of those who are faithful to God: "Here is the patience of the saints; here are those who keep the commandments of God and the faith of Jesus" (Revelation 14:12).

This is what the first angel was talking about with the "everlasting gospel," which is what the "faith of Jesus" is all about. When we have faith in Jesus and trust in Him, our sins are forgiven and we stand perfect before God.

At the same time, these people are depicted as those who keep "the commandments of God." Those commandments call us to worship the Creator, have no idols and keep the Sabbath in memorial of God as Creator. If you have the faith of Jesus and are keeping God's commandments, there is no way you could be worshipping "the beast and his image."

Almost everything we have looked at in this book culminates here, in God's final warning message to the world.

WHEN THE PARTY IS OVER

Years ago, a police organisation was trying to bug a mobster's headquarters. The problem was that the grounds were patrolled by five or six big, vicious Doberman Pinschers. The police couldn't think of a way to get around them.

One of the cops decided to try hamburgers. At first, they would throw the burgers to the dogs through the fence and they would stop barking long enough to scoff down the food. The cops did this night after night until, eventually, the formerly-vicious dogs were eating right out of the policemen's hands. One night, while the dogs were feasting, the police team was able to get into the headquarters and place the bugging devices where they needed to be.

Of course, once the bugs were placed, they stopped feeding the dogs and the party was over.

We've been given a warning. Should we listen or get caught up in a "feast" that is going to end sooner or later? If we are deceived and find ourselves on the wrong side of the great controversy, we end up with nothing. In contrast, God offers us everything He originally had planned for us.

beyond **commitment**

As a young man in Mississippi, American author William Faulkner worked at the local post office. He wasn't really suited to the job and admitted that he hated it. While at the office, he'd invite friends over. They would sit around drinking tea, playing cards and reading the magazines that were supposed to go to the subscribers.

One customer complained that when he wasn't getting his mail, he found some of it stuffed in a trashcan behind the post office.

After his boss had finally had enough, young Faulkner was fired. When he left, the aspiring young writer told his best friend:

> I reckon I'll be at the beck and call of folks with money my whole life, but thank God I won't ever again have to be at the beck and call of every [blank of a blank] whose got two cents to buy a postage stamp.

It doesn't sound like he had much commitment.

British writer and philosopher Bertrand Russell told how he was riding his bicycle out in the country one day when it suddenly struck him that he no longer loved his wife. So he went home and ended the marriage, just like that.

Where was his commitment to his wife?

Of course, commitment isn't always positive. Many of the problems in this world are caused by people committed to what is not good. As previously mentioned, one only has to think of suicide bombers—those who blow themselves up, hoping to kill as many of us in the process as possible. We might hate what they do and what they stand for but you can't deny that they are committed.

Commitment reminds me of the lines from William Butler Yeats's poem, "The Second Coming":

> Things fall apart; the centre cannot hold;
> Mere anarchy is loosed upon the world,
> The blood-dimmed tide is loosed, and everywhere
> The ceremony of innocence is drowned;
> The best lack all conviction, while the worst
> Are full of passionate intensity.

Commitment—loyalty to a cause in and of itself—isn't necessarily a good thing. What really matters is the cause itself.

THE MOST OUTRAGEOUS CLAIM

In this book, we've been considering some heavy ideas and themes.

While Star Wars may be fiction, it was onto something with this notion of a universal battle between good and evil. We don't just see this battle played out in the larger scheme of things, like war, crime and blatant cases of good versus evil. Such cases include attempts to stop child porn or to end the trafficking of women forced into prostitution. But we also see this struggle played out in our own lives. We are all in this struggle and, what's more, we're all on one side or the other.

Either these are the most ridiculous lies ever promoted by human beings, or they are the most important life-changing truths anyone could ever know. If true, they answer so many of the tough questions about life: Who are we? How did we get here? Why are we here? Why does suffering exist? What is our ultimate fate? Is death the end of it all?

The claim isn't just that God exists as a Creator God who made the universe. The outrageous claim is that this God—the One who created everything that was created—shrank down and took on Himself our humanity. While in the form of humanity, He gave Himself as a sacrifice for our bad deeds and wrong choices in the great controversy we are now living in, so we don't have to perish and can live forever in an ideal world.

The visible universe is something like 157,000,000,000 light years large. What we are claiming is that the One who created this universe—the visible and invisible parts—is the One who, Himself, is greater than the universe. He has to be greater than it in order to create it and He is the hero, Jesus of Nazareth.

Consider what the Bible says about Jesus:

- "Inasmuch then as the children have partaken of flesh and blood, He [Jesus] Himself likewise shared in the same, that through death He might destroy him who had the power of death, that is, the devil" (Hebrews 2:14).

- "In the beginning was the Word, and the Word was with God, and the Word was God. . . . All things were made through Him, and without Him nothing was made that was made. . . . He was in the world, and the world was made through Him, and the world did not know Him" (John 1:1, 3, 10).

- "Let this mind be in you which was also in Christ Jesus, who, being in the form of God, did not consider it robbery to be equal with God, but made Himself of no reputation, taking the form of a bondservant, and coming in the likeness of men. And being found in appearance as a man, He humbled Himself and became obedient to the point of death, even the death of the cross" (Philippians 2:5–8).

If you could believe what these verses are saying, what else really matters?

Some people tell us we are products of mere chance, born into a cold, uncaring universe. Reflecting on this perspective, French biologist Jacques Monod wrote:

> The ancient covenant is in pieces; man knows at last that he is alone in the universe's unfeeling immensity, out of which he emerged only by chance. His destiny is nowhere spelled out, nor is his duty. The kingdom above or the darkness below; it is for him to choose.

But where is this "kingdom above" and how can we "choose" it in a universe where, according to Monod, we are alone? If we arose solely by chance, where could we find this "kingdom" in the universe he described?

His view is in radical contrast to these famous verses:

> For God so loved the world that He gave His only begotten Son, that whoever believes in Him should not perish but have everlasting life. For God did not send His Son into the world to condemn the world, but that the world through Him might be saved (John 3:16, 17).

What do we do with this information? If you can believe it—if you do believe it—this changes everything.

THE FALERII FACTOR

A young man was wrestling with the question of the existence of God. Though an atheist, he thought that if God existed, then nothing could be the same. He'd have to learn about this God, why He created us and what He wanted from us. In the end, the young man came to believe not only that God existed but that this God died for him as well.

And, indeed, his life completely changed.

How could it not?

Imagine for a minute that you are a doctor. You get sick but there is medicine you have access to. You fully understand how it works, what it does to the body and how it brings healing. You understand it in ways that few people ever could. In fact, let's say you were the one who created that medication. All the knowledge in the world isn't going to make it work for you unless you take it yourself.

The classical writer Plutarch of Chaeronea told of the Roman siege of a city called Falerii. It was a well fortified city and the inhabitants didn't seem concerned about the Romans outside. At times, they would even venture outside the walls. The Roman outposts were far enough away that the Falerii felt safe outside—but not too far from the walls.

According to Plutarch, a schoolteacher started taking the children outside the walls. At first, they stayed close but, over time, he purposely took them further and further out. The children would play, exercise and have fun, day after day. He continued to do this until he got them far enough away to deliver them into the hands of the Romans. He asked to see the commander of the troops, a leader named Marcus Furius Camillus. He presented the children to him, knowing this would force the people inside the city to surrender because the Romans had their children as captives.

What happened next was fascinating, as Camillus railed against the schoolteacher's treachery. He said that though war often brought injustices and evils, some things were just not done—and a betrayal like this was one of them.

"A great general," he said, "should rely on his own virtue, and not on other men's vices."

One can only imagine what the parents of Falerii thought when they discovered the treachery. Expecting the worst, they must have been amazed when they saw the schoolteacher, naked and bound, being led back to the city by the children. They shouted out praises to Camillus, calling him their "preserver, god and father."

Stunned by the treachery, yet so appreciative of what Camillus had done for them, the city immediately turned itself over to his rule. Overwhelmed by the virtue and justice of his act, they submitted themselves to him.

Though just an analogy, this story shows what a new life in Christ is all about. You get a glimpse of who you really are and what your situation really is. It helps you understand what Christ has done for you and what He is offering you.

Then if you are open—seeking to know truth, seeking answers and help, and seeking something you can never attain by yourself—you will be led to a whole new existence in Christ. All you have to do is give yourself over to Him, asking Him to heal our brokenness and to influence our daily lives.

DEAD END

The early Beatniks existed before there were hippies—the "free love" generation of the 1960s and 1970s. They even had their own Bible of sorts, a novel by Jean-Louise "Jack" Kerouac called *On the Road*. The book is all about a bunch of guys who travel around the United States drinking, taking drugs and partying.

Listen to these lines from the book:

> I have travelled eight thousand miles around the American continent, and I was back in Times Square and right in the middle of rush hour, too, seeing with my innocent road eyes the absolute madness and fantastic hoorair of New York with millions and millions hustling forever for a buck among themselves, the mad dream—grabbing, taking, giving, sighing, dying, just so they could be buried in those awful cemetery cities beyond Long Island City.

The novel was based on real-life characters, most of which ended up dying of drugs or going to jail. Theirs wasn't a "happily-ever-after ending." Their life on the road became a dead end.

The irony is that Kerouac always insisted the Beats were a religious generation. He insisted that they were on a spiritual quest—a quest for meaning, answers, hope and something beyond ending up in one of "those awful cemetery cities beyond Long Island City."

Whether they ever reached it is another story though. Hope isn't found by staring at the bottom of an empty Tequila bottle.

The Beats represent what we all are looking for in this life: a hope for something we sense we need, want and strive for, yet can't put our fingers on. This hope can be found, experienced and known by each of us personally if we're willing to make a radical, life-changing commitment to Jesus.

In the end, we're all committed to something, even if it's nothing more than our own passions and lusts. Whatever it is, whether it's money or self love, it's destined for oblivion.

If that is all we have to commit to, why not commit to something that offers us an alternative?

> For all that is in the world—the lust of the flesh, the lust of the eyes, and the pride of life—is not of the Father but is of the world. And the world is passing away, and the lust of it; but he who does the will of God abides forever (1 John 2:16, 17).

BAPTISM

Though the phrase has sometimes taken on bad connotations, it's what is known as being "born again." You get a fresh start—that means a new beginning and a chance to start over:

> Therefore we were buried with Him through baptism into death, that just as Christ was raised from the dead by the glory of the Father, even so we also should walk in newness of life (Romans 6:4).

This is talking about baptism. In the earliest Christian tradition, this involves lowering a person under water as a symbolic and public expression of commitment. It's an act that recognises that "you gotta serve somebody"—as Dylan put it—and that this Somebody is the Jesus who offers this new life.

The act of baptism is a symbolic death to your old ways of living and begins a new life of commitment and love to God. It's an amazing experience to both come to believe in God, and get to know and love Him.

In the 1968 Olympics, one poor marathon runner limped across the finish line long after everyone else had finished. He finally came to the line more than an hour after the last runner. When he was asked why he didn't give up, he replied, "My country did not send me to Mexico City to start the race; they sent me to finish the race."

That runner showed real commitment to his sport and his country. How much more committed should we be to God, the One who created us, died for us, offers us eternal life and made a way for us to escape the inevitable destruction we all face?

Davy came back from a war, badly disfigured from where a grenade had blown up and ripped his face to shreds. When he looked in the mirror, he saw a monster. In the next bed was another soldier, also badly disfigured from a wound. He listened as this soldier's wife announced that she wanted a divorce. Davy felt a shudder of incredible anguish go through him. What would his wife say when she came in and saw him for the first time?

When she arrived, she walked into the room and showed no surprise at his appearance. Instead, she walked up and kissed what was left of his face. Smiling, she said, "Welcome home, Davey! I love you."

It's the same as what God does for us. No matter how messed up we are or how "disfigured"—emotionally, physically and spiritually—He loves us and accepts us.

Throughout the Bible, the image of marriage is used to describe the ideal relationship between God and His people. You marry someone because you want to share your life together. You want to give your whole self to that person, and be close and intimate. You love that person and they love you, so your life is never the same again.

Of course, we hear sad stories of infidelity in marriage all the time. The difference is that God will never be unfaithful to us.

If infidelity arises, it's on our side. But the good news is that God will always take us back, forgive us and give us another chance. It's what we looked at earlier—grace. Without grace, we would be lost.

No marriage is perfect and no relationship with God is perfect. We will make mistakes, both with our spouse in marriage and in our relationship with God. But just as God forgives us, we also learn to forgive our partners. No marriage would work without learning to forgive each other. And just as God accepts us as we are, we need to learn to accept our spouses as they are in marriage.

NEW DIRECTIONS

In some ways, the marriage analogy breaks down, though. How often have you heard one spouse say about another, "I've been trying to change him for 20 years and it hasn't worked"?

The good news is that God does change us. Having a new life in Him means having a changed life. It means we become different people in Him. We may not suddenly become angels but our lives move in entirely new directions. When faced with situations in life, we start to make different kinds of choices than we would have before.

Like the citizens of Falerii, we choose to change our allegiances. We become committed to God, which involves making new choices based on what the Bible says God's will is for our lives.

As we have noted, what God asks us to do is for our own good. Who hasn't looked back and regretted a bad choice or two—choices that we wouldn't have made if we had been seeking to obey the Lord and His law?

God will accept you as you are but He wants to change you for the better. He can only do that to the degree you surrender to Him. Central to this surrender are the choices we make.

NO TEMPTATION

Big-wave surfing isn't just a sport—it's a discipline and a way of life. You have to be prepared, dedicated and able to take care of yourself to do this and manage to survive!

It's probably even more dangerous than it looks. In a big-wave wipe-out, a breaking wave can push surfers 15 metres below the surface. Once they stop spinning around, they have to quickly regain their equilibrium and figure out which way is up.

Surfers may have less than 20 seconds to get back to the top before the next big wave hits them. Even worse, the water pressure at those depths can rupture your eardrums. The current and force of the water at those depths can slam a surfer into a reef or the ocean floor, resulting in severe injuries or even death.

One of the greatest risks is being held underwater by two or more consecutive waves. Surviving "a triple hold-down" is extremely difficult and surfers have to be in top shape to deal with things like this.

These people have to make choices that reflect their commitment to what they do. If they weren't committed to surfing, they wouldn't do it.

It's the same with being a Christian. God loves us and He wants what's best for us. But what we've seen in this whole great controversy scenario is that God does not force us. Even when we give our lives to Him, we still have to make our own choices. When we do make them, God offers us power and strength to make the right decisions. But the choice is always ours.

> No temptation has overtaken you except such as is common to man; but God is faithful, who will not allow you to be tempted beyond what you are able, but with the temptation will also make the way of escape, that you may be able to bear it (1 Corinthians 10:13).

Look at this world and all of the ruined lives in it. Life was never meant to be this way but love requires freedom to be love. Freedom involves risks and this sad, painful world is the result.

But it isn't going to last forever. It's all going to be redone, reworked and made over to be as it was originally meant to be. A part of this process begins now, with what God does for us in our lives. But God can only help us when we cooperate and allow Him to.

Big-wave surfers have to train, prepare and commit to what they do. If they don't they will get swept away and, perhaps, never be found again.

We are all being swept along in something much bigger and more powerful than ocean waves. Our lives are part of this great epic—this great controversy between good and evil. We're in a battle we cannot win by ourselves.

Jesus is our hero, the One who won the decisive victory for us. With His victory comes the hope and promise that we can share in that victory with Him. He offers it to us, but we have to make the choice to accept it. If we do, our lives will be changed forever.

Why not see what Jesus has to offer?

It will change your life—for the better!

Watch the award winning series that explores life's biggest questions

Uncover an epic story that gives new perspective to the conflict, pain and confusion of this world. Beyond the Search finds meaning in the big picture and gives hope to a world in crisis.

www.beyond.info